A VE
LEVEL

4



# MATHEMATICS

By Richard Cooper

RISING STARS

PLEASE NOTE: THIS BOOK MAY NOT BE PHOTOCOPIED OR REPRODUCED AND WE APPRECIATE YOUR HELP IN PROTECTING OUR COPYRIGHT.

Rising Stars UK Ltd, 22 Grafton Street, London W1S 4EX

www.risingstars-uk.com



First published 2003
This edition 2007



Editorial: Tanya Solomons
Design: Clive Sutherland
Cover design: Burville-Riley Design
Illustrations: Burville-Riley Design, Beehive Illustration (Theresa Tibbetts) and Ken Vail Graphic Design
Cover image: Beehive Illustration (Theresa Tibbetts)



British Library Cataloguing in Publication Data
A CIP record for this book is available from the British Library.

ISBN 978-1-84680-114-3

Printed by Craft Print International Ltd, Singapore

# Contents

# How to use this book

## What we have included:

Those topics at Level 3 that are trickiest to get right.
ALL Level 4 content so you know that you are covering all the topics that could come up in the test.

1. **Introduction section** – This section tells you what you need to do to get a Level 4. It picks out the key learning objective and explains it simply to you.

2. **Self assessment** – Colour in the face that best describes your understanding of this concept.

3. **Question** – The question helps you to learn by doing. It is presented in a similar way to a SATs question and gives you a real example to work with.

4. **Flow chart** – This shows you the steps to use when completing questions like this.

This icon indicates the section is a *teaching* section.

5. **Tip boxes** – These provide test hints and general tips on getting the best marks in the SATs.

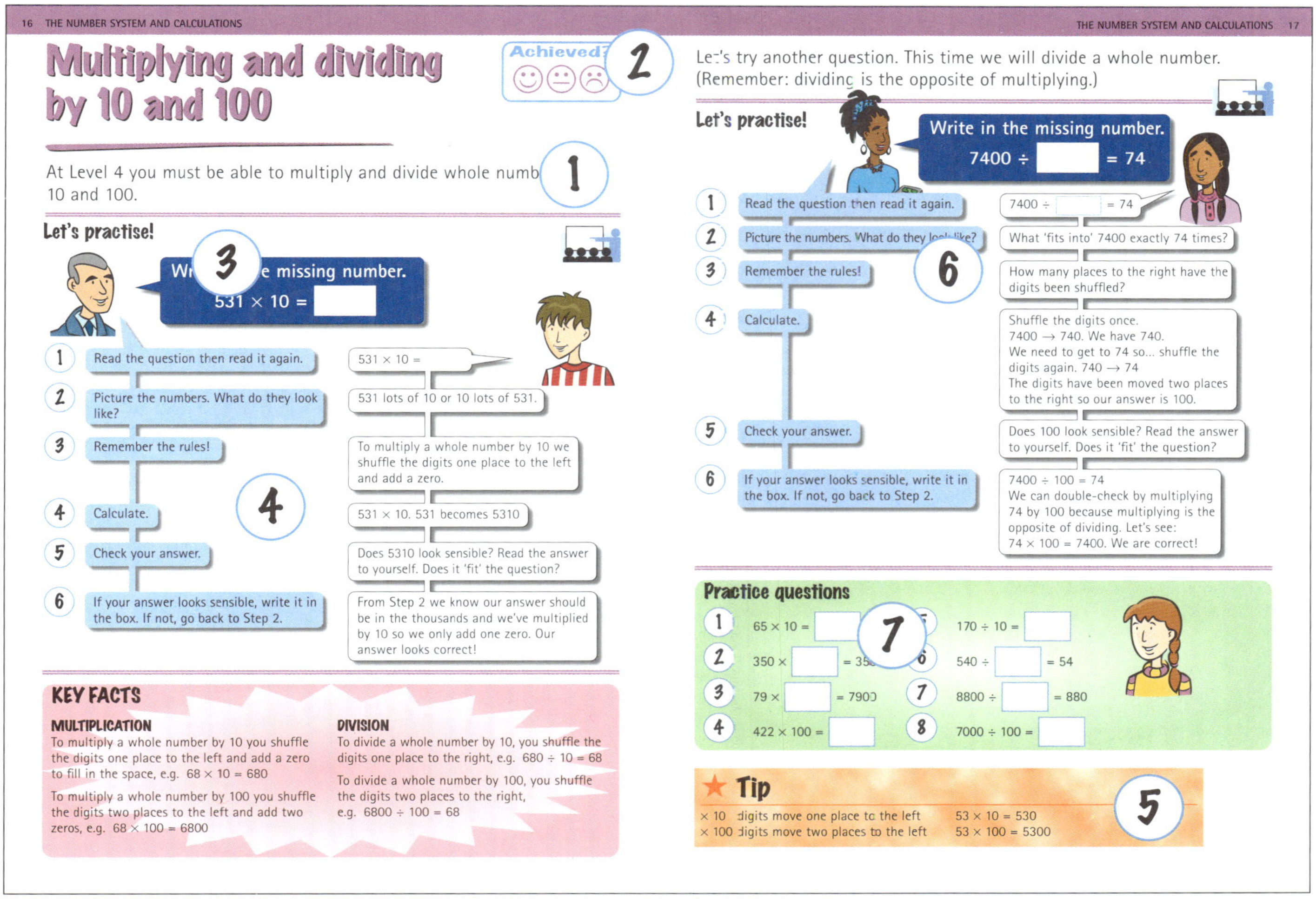
16 THE NUMBER SYSTEM AND CALCULATIONS

# Multiplying and dividing by 10 and 100

Achieved? 2

At Level 4 you must be able to multiply and divide whole numb 1
10 and 100.

**Let's practise!**

Wr 3 e missing number.
531 × 10 =

1 Read the question then read it again. — 531 × 10 =
2 Picture the numbers. What do they look like? — 531 lots of 10 or 10 lots of 531.
3 Remember the rules! — To multiply a whole number by 10 we shuffle the digits one place to the left and add a zero.
4 Calculate. — 531 × 10. 531 becomes 5310
5 Check your answer. — Does 5310 look sensible? Read the answer to yourself. Does it 'fit' the question?
6 If your answer looks sensible, write it in the box. If not, go back to Step 2. — From Step 2 we know our answer should be in the thousands and we've multiplied by 10 so we only add one zero. Our answer looks correct!

4

**KEY FACTS**

**MULTIPLICATION**
To multiply a whole number by 10 you shuffle the digits one place to the left and add a zero to fill in the space, e.g. 68 × 10 = 680
To multiply a whole number by 100 you shuffle the digits two places to the left and add two zeros, e.g. 68 × 100 = 6800

**DIVISION**
To divide a whole number by 10, you shuffle the digits one place to the right, e.g. 680 ÷ 10 = 68
To divide a whole number by 100, you shuffle the digits two places to the right, e.g. 6800 ÷ 100 = 68

THE NUMBER SYSTEM AND CALCULATIONS 17

Let's try another question. This time we will divide a whole number. (Remember: dividing is the opposite of multiplying.)

**Let's practise!**

Write in the missing number.
7400 ÷ ☐ = 74

1 Read the question then read it again. — 7400 ÷ ☐ = 74
2 Picture the numbers. What do they look like? — What 'fits into' 7400 exactly 74 times?
3 Remember the rules! — How many places to the right have the digits been shuffled?
4 Calculate. — Shuffle the digits once. 7400 → 740. We have 740. We need to get to 74 so... shuffle the digits again. 740 → 74. The digits have been moved two places to the right so our answer is 100.
5 Check your answer. — Does 100 look sensible? Read the answer to yourself. Does it 'fit' the question?
6 If your answer looks sensible, write it in the box. If not, go back to Step 2. — 7400 ÷ 100 = 74. We can double-check by multiplying 74 by 100 because multiplying is the opposite of dividing. Let's see: 74 × 100 = 7400. We are correct!

6

**Practice questions** 7

1 65 × 10 = ☐
2 350 × ☐ = 35..
3 79 × ☐ = 7900
4 422 × 100 = ☐
5 170 ÷ 10 = ☐
6 540 ÷ ☐ = 54
7 8800 ÷ ☐ = 880
8 7000 ÷ 100 = ☐

**Tip**
× 10 digits move one place to the left — 53 × 10 = 530
× 100 digits move two places to the left — 53 × 100 = 5300

5

6 **Second question** – On most pages there will be a second question. This will either look at a slightly different question type or give you another example to work through.

7 **Practice questions** – This is where you have to do the work! Try the question using the technique in the flow chart then check your answers at the back. Practising questions is the best way to help improve your understanding.

We have also put in a big selection of our favourite test techniques, tips for revision and some advice on what the National Tests are all about, as well as the answers so you can see how well you are getting on.

**GOOD LUCK!**

# Achieve Level 4 Maths – Objectives

This chart allows you to see the progression from Year 5 to Year 6 for each strand following the New Primary Mathematics Framework.

The key objectives are in **bold type**.

| Strand | Year 5 | Year 6 |
| --- | --- | --- |
| Using and applying mathematics | Solve one-step and two-step problems involving whole numbers and decimals and all four operations, choosing and using appropriate calculation strategies, including calculator use | Solve multi-step problems, and problems involving fractions, decimals and percentages; choose and use appropriate calculation strategies at each stage, including calculator use |
| | Represent a puzzle or problem by identifying and recording the information or calculations needed to solve it; find possible solutions and confirm them in the context of the problem | Tabulate systematically the information in a problem or puzzle; identify and record the steps or calculations needed to solve it, using symbols where appropriate; interpret solutions in the original context and check their accuracy |
| | Plan and pursue an enquiry; present evidence by collecting, organising and interpreting information; suggest extensions to the enquiry | Suggest, plan and develop lines of enquiry; collect, organise and represent information, interpret results and review methods; identify and answer related questions |
| | Explore patterns, properties and relationships and propose a general statement involving numbers or shapes; identify examples for which the statement is true or false | Represent and interpret sequences, patterns and relationships involving numbers and shapes; suggest and test hypotheses; construct and use simple expressions and formulae in words then symbols (e.g. the cost of c pens at 15 pence each is 15c pence) |
| | Explain reasoning using diagrams, graphs and text; refine ways of recording using images and symbols | Explain reasoning and conclusions, using words, symbols or diagrams as appropriate |
| Counting and understanding number | Count from any given number in whole-number and decimal steps, extending beyond zero when counting backwards; relate the numbers to their position on a number line | Find the difference between a positive and a negative integer, or two negative integers, in context |
| | **Explain what each digit represents in whole numbers and decimals with up to two places, and partition, round and order these numbers** | Use decimal notation for tenths, hundredths and thousandths; partition, round and order decimals with up to three places, and position them on the number line |
| | Express a smaller whole number as a fraction of a larger one (e.g. recognise that 5 out of 8 is $\frac{5}{8}$); find equivalent fractions (e.g. $\frac{7}{10} = \frac{14}{20}$, or $\frac{19}{10} = 1\frac{9}{10}$); relate fractions to their decimal representations | Express a larger whole number as a fraction of a smaller one (e.g. recognise that 8 slices of a 5-slice pizza represents $\frac{8}{5}$ or $1\frac{3}{5}$ pizzas); simplify fractions by cancelling common factors; order a set of fractions by converting them to fractions with a common denominator |
| | Understand percentage as the number of parts in every 100 and express tenths and hundredths as percentages | **Express one quantity as a percentage of another (e.g. express £400 as a percentage of £1000); find equivalent percentages, decimals and fractions** |
| | Use sequences to scale numbers up or down; solve problems involving proportions of quantities (e.g. decrease quantities in a recipe designed to feed six people) | Solve simple problems involving direct proportion by scaling quantities up or down |
| Knowing and using number facts | **Use knowledge of place value and addition and subtraction of two-digit numbers to derive sums and differences and doubles and halves of decimals (e.g. 6.5 ± 2.7, half of 5.6, double 0.34)** | **Use knowledge of place value and multiplication facts to 10 x 10 to derive related multiplication and division facts involving decimals (e.g. 0.8 x 7, 4.8 ÷ 6)** |
| | Recall quickly multiplication facts up to 10 x 10 and use them to multiply pairs of multiples of 10 and 100; derive quickly corresponding division facts | Use knowledge of multiplication facts to derive quickly squares of numbers to 12 x 12 and the corresponding squares of multiples of 10 |
| | Identify pairs of factors of two-digit whole numbers and find common multiples (e.g. for 6 and 9) | Recognise that prime numbers have only two factors and identify prime numbers less than 100; find the prime factors of two-digit numbers |
| | Use knowledge of rounding, place value, number facts and inverse operations to estimate and check calculations | Use approximations, inverse operations and tests of divisibility to estimate and check results |

| Strand | Year 5 | Year 6 |
|---|---|---|
| Calculating | Extend mental methods for whole-number calculations, for example to multiply a two-digit by a one-digit number (e.g. 12 x 9), to multiply by 25 (e.g. 16 x 25), to subtract one near multiple of 1000 from another (e.g. 6070 – 4097) | Calculate mentally with integers and decimals: U.t ± U.t, TU x U, TU ÷ U, U.t x U, U.t ÷ U |
| | **Use efficient written methods to add and subtract whole numbers and decimals with up to two places** | **Use efficient written methods to add and subtract integers and decimals, to multiply and divide integers and decimals by a one digit integer, and to multiply two-digit and three-digit integers by a two-digit integer** |
| | Use understanding of place value to multiply and divide whole numbers and decimals by 10, 100 or 1000 | Relate fractions to multiplication and division (e.g. 6 ÷ 2 = $\frac{1}{2}$ of 6 = 6 x $\frac{1}{2}$); express a quotient as a fraction or decimal (e.g. 67 ÷ 5 = 13.4 or $13\frac{2}{5}$); find fractions and percentages of whole-number quantities (e.g. $\frac{5}{8}$ of 96, 65% of £260) |
| | Refine and use efficient written methods to multiply and divide HTU x U, TU ? TU, U.t x U and HTU ÷ U | Use a calculator to solve problems involving multi-step calculations |
| | Find fractions using division (e.g. $\frac{1}{100}$ of 5 kg), and percentages of numbers and quantities (e.g. 10%, 5% and 15% of £80) | |
| | Use a calculator to solve problems, including those involving decimals or fractions (e.g. find $\frac{3}{4}$ of 150 g); interpret the display correctly in the context of measurement | |
| Understanding shape | Identify, visualise and describe properties of rectangles, triangles, regular polygons and 3-D solids; use knowledge of properties to draw 2-D shapes, and to identify and draw nets of 3-D shapes | Describe, identify and visualise parallel and perpendicular edges or faces; use these properties to classify 2-D shapes and 3-D solids |
| | **Read and plot coordinates in the first quadrant; recognise parallel and perpendicular lines in grids and shapes; use a set-square and ruler to draw shapes with perpendicular or parallel sides** | Make and draw shapes with increasing accuracy and apply knowledge of their properties |
| | Complete patterns with up to two lines of symmetry; draw the position of a shape after a reflection or translation | **Visualise and draw on grids of different types where a shape will be after reflection, after translations, or after rotation through 90° or 180° about its centre or one of its vertices** |
| | Estimate, draw and measure acute and obtuse angles using an angle measurer or protractor to a suitable degree of accuracy; calculate angles in a straight line | Use coordinates in the first quadrant to draw, locate and complete shapes that meet given properties |
| | | Estimate angles, and use a protractor to measure and draw them, on their own and in shapes; calculate angles in a triangle or around a point |
| Measuring | Read, choose, use and record standard metric units to estimate and measure length, weight and capacity to a suitable degree of accuracy (e.g. the nearest centimetre); convert larger to smaller units using decimals to one place (e.g. change 2.6 kg to 2600 g) | **Select and use standard metric units of measure and convert between units using decimals to two places (e.g. change 2.75 litres to 2750 ml, or vice versa)** |
| | Interpret a reading that lies between two unnumbered divisions on a scale | Read and interpret scales on a range of measuring instruments, recognising that the measurement made is approximate and recording results to a required degree of accuracy; compare readings on different scales, for example when using different instruments |
| | **Draw and measure lines to the nearest millimetre; measure and calculate the perimeter of regular and irregular polygons; use the formula for the area of a rectangle to calculate the rectangle's area** | Calculate the perimeter and area of rectilinear shapes; estimate the area of an irregular shape by counting squares |
| | Read timetables and time using 24-hour clock notation; use a calendar to calculate time intervals | |
| Handling data | Describe the occurrence of familiar events using the language of chance or likelihood | Describe and predict outcomes from data using the language of chance or likelihood |
| | Answer a set of related questions by collecting, selecting and organising relevant data; draw conclusions, using ICT to present features, and identify further questions to ask | **Solve problems by collecting, selecting, processing, presenting and interpreting data, using ICT where appropriate; draw conclusions and identify further questions to ask** |
| | **Construct frequency tables, pictograms and bar and line graphs to represent the frequencies of events and changes over time** | Construct and interpret frequency tables, bar charts with grouped discrete data, and line graphs; interpret pie charts |
| | Find and interpret the mode of a set of data | Describe and interpret results and solutions to problems using the mode, range, median and mean |

# Decimal notation and negative numbers

Achieved? ☺ 😐 ☹

## Money

A good way to understand more about decimals is to work with money. We use pounds and pence. There are one hundred pence in one pound.

We use 'decimal notation' to record money.

Three pounds fifty pence is written like this.

On the left of the decimal point is the number of whole pounds.

On the right of the decimal point is the number of pence or fractions of a whole pound.

number of pounds — number of pence

**£3.50**

pound sign — decimal point separating pounds and pence

For each of these amounts, write the number of pounds and number of pence.

1. £7.42
   ________ pounds
   ________ pence
2. £14.28
   ________ pounds
   ________ pence
3. £53.71
   ________ pounds
   ________ pence
4. £109.86
   ________ pounds
   ________ pence
5. £426.19
   ________ pounds
   ________ pence

## Temperature

Negative numbers are numbers below zero. Thermometers measure temperature and use numbers below zero when it is freezing (0°).

(a)
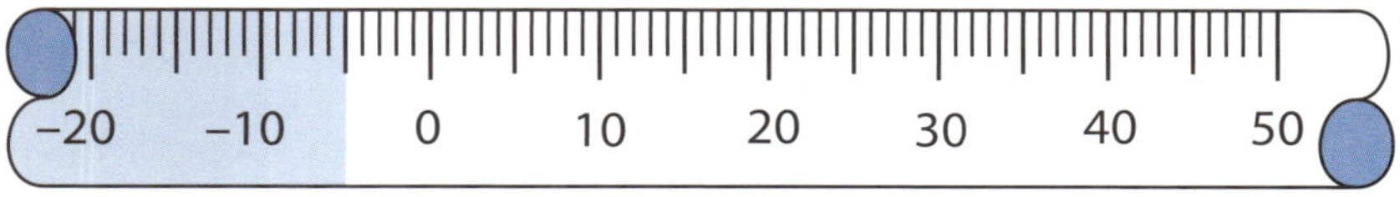

The temperature is -5° or 5 degrees below zero.

(b)
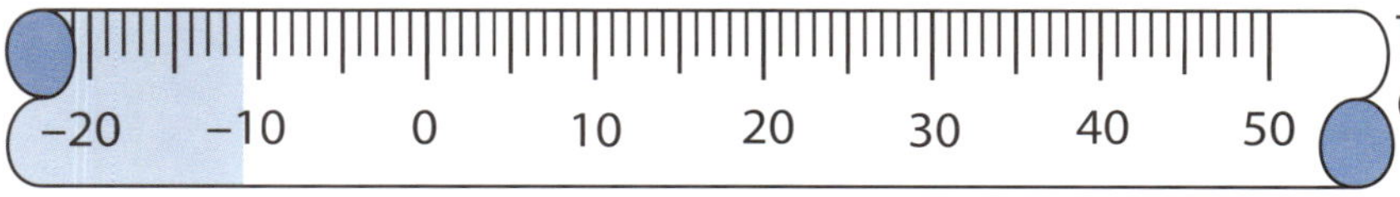

The temperature is -11° or 11 degrees below zero.

Which do you think is colder? (a) ☐ (b) ☐

### ★ Tip 1

When writing the number of pence ALWAYS put in the zeros.

For example: £3.05 ✓ £7.40 ✓
£3.5 ✗ £7.4 ✗

### ★ Tip 2

Don't forget to include zero when counting up and down a temperature scale.
Think of a thermometer like a number line.
The greater the negative number on a thermometer, the colder it is.

# Subtraction

Achieved? ☺ 😐 ☹

## Written subtractions

You will be able to do some sums easily in your head (e.g. 200 – 100). Others are a bit harder and you may need a paper and pencil.

## Let's practise!

Write in the missing number.

749 – 365 = ☐

1. Estimate first.

   750 – 350. Our answer will be around 400.

2. Write the digits neatly in their columns.

   $$\begin{array}{r} \text{H T U} \\ 7\;4\;9 \\ -\;3\;6\;5 \\ \hline \\ \hline \end{array}$$

3. Start with the units, then the tens, then the hundreds. If the top number is smaller than the bottom number, then exchange across from the next column.

   $$\begin{array}{r} \text{H T U} \\ {}^{6}\not{7}\;{}^{1}4\;9 \\ -\;3\;6\;5 \\ \hline 8\;4 \\ \hline \end{array}$$

   In the tens column, the top number (4) is smaller than the bottom number (6) so we need to exchange from the hundreds column. 14 – 6 = 8

4. Now do the digits in the hundreds column to complete your answer.

   $$\begin{array}{r} \text{H T U} \\ {}^{6}\not{7}\;{}^{1}4\;9 \\ -\;3\;6\;5 \\ \hline 3\;8\;4 \\ \hline \end{array}$$

   6 – 3 = 3

5. Does your answer look sensible?

   Yes, the estimate was 400.

## Practice questions

Try these. Round up or down to estimate your answer first.

1. 443 – 372 = ☐
2. 795 – 628 = ☐
3. 482 – 336 = ☐
4. 910 – 772 = ☐
5. 835 – 671 = ☐
6. 655 – 556 = ☐

### ★ Tip

Work step-by-step starting with the units and work towards the left hand side.

### ★ Tip

Don't forget that you can check the answer to a subtraction by using addition.

# 2, 3, 4, 5 and 10 times tables

To achieve Level 4 you will need to know and be able to use all these table facts.

| 2 times table | 3 times table | 4 times table | 5 times table | 10 times table |
|---|---|---|---|---|
| 1 × 2 = 2 | 1 × 3 = 3 | 1 × 4 = 4 | 1 × 5 = 5 | 1 × 10 = 10 |
| 2 × 2 = 4 | 2 × 3 = 6 | 2 × 4 = 8 | 2 × 5 = 10 | 2 × 10 = 20 |
| 3 × 2 = 6 | 3 × 3 = 9 | 3 × 4 = 12 | 3 × 5 = 15 | 3 × 10 = 30 |
| 4 × 2 = 8 | 4 × 3 = 12 | 4 × 4 = 16 | 4 × 5 = 20 | 4 × 10 = 40 |
| 5 × 2 = 10 | 5 × 3 = 15 | 5 × 4 = 20 | 5 × 5 = 25 | 5 × 10 = 50 |
| 6 × 2 = 12 | 6 × 3 = 18 | 6 × 4 = 24 | 6 × 5 = 30 | 6 × 10 = 60 |
| 7 × 2 = 14 | 7 × 3 = 21 | 7 × 4 = 28 | 7 × 5 = 35 | 7 × 10 = 70 |
| 8 × 2 = 16 | 8 × 3 = 24 | 8 × 4 = 32 | 8 × 5 = 40 | 8 × 10 = 80 |
| 9 × 2 = 18 | 9 × 3 = 27 | 9 × 4 = 36 | 9 × 5 = 45 | 9 × 10 = 90 |
| 10 × 2 = 20 | 10 × 3 = 30 | 10 × 4 = 40 | 10 × 5 = 50 | 10 × 10 = 100 |

**★ Tip 1**
Answers are always even numbers.

**★ Tip 2**
The digits, when added together, make 3, 6 or 9.

**★ Tip 3**
The answers are double the 2 times table.

**★ Tip 4**
The answers always end in 5 or 0.

**★ Tip 5**
The answers always end in 0.

## Using tables facts to help with division sums

Remember, division is the **inverse** or **opposite** of multiplication. For example:

$$5 \times 4 = 20 \text{ so } 20 \div 4 = 5$$

### Practice questions

Use the multiplication tables to complete these division facts.

1. 12 ÷ 6 = ☐
2. 28 ÷ 4 = ☐
3. ☐ ÷ 7 = 10
4. 36 ÷ 4 = ☐
5. 25 ÷ ☐ = 5
6. ☐ ÷ 2 = 7
7. 16 ÷ ☐ = 2
8. ☐ ÷ 10 = 8
9. 36 ÷ 6 = ☐
10. ☐ ÷ 4 = 8
11. 40 ÷ ☐ = 8
12. 20 ÷ 4 = ☐
13. ☐ ÷ 2 = 3
14. 4 ÷ 4 = ☐
15. 21 ÷ 3 = ☐

# Number problems

Number problems often 'hide' the maths behind the words.
Follow our step-by-step guide to achieve success!

## Let's practise!

**Harvey has 4 football stickers. Oona has 6 times as many football stickers as Harvey. How many stickers does Oona have?**

1. Read the question then read it again.
2. Picture the numbers.
3. Decide which operation to use and calculate.
4. Read the question and answer. What were you asked to do? Is your answer sensible?

This is really important. There are lots of words in this question.

4 6

**6 times as many**
That means multiply ...
Harvey has 4 stickers so $4 \times 6 = 24$.

How many stickers does Oona have?
Oona has 24 stickers.

Number problems involving division might not have answers that fit exactly. They may have remainders. You have to decide whether to round the answer up or down.

**Miss Banks has 29 children in her class. A table seats 4 children. How many tables does she need to seat all the children?**

1. Read the question then read it again.
2. Picture the numbers.
3. Decide which operation to use and calculate.
4. Round up or round down?

29 4

**How many tables to seat the children?**
It's division. $29 \div 4 = 7$ r1

Up... so 8 tables are needed to seat all the children. Otherwise 1 would be standing.

# Equivalent fractions

Achieved?

To achieve Level 4 you will need to be able to use fractions that are parts of a whole and recognise when two fractions are equivalent.

**KEY FACTS**

A fraction is 'part of a number'.

A quarter or $\frac{1}{4}$ means 1 part out of 4 equal parts. One quarter of this diagram has been shaded.

Three quarters or $\frac{3}{4}$ means 3 parts out of 4 equal parts. Three quarters of this diagram have been shaded.

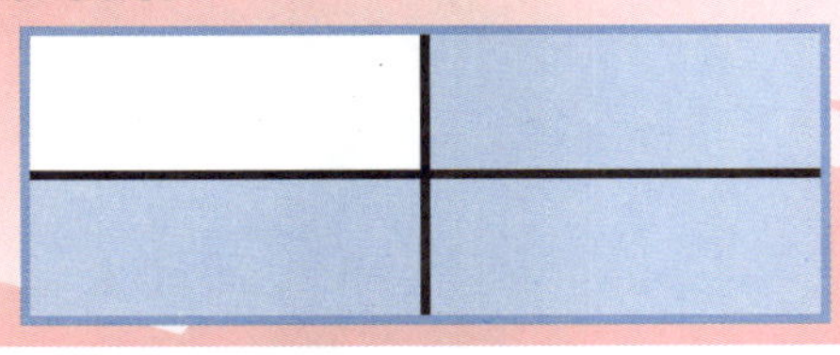

Have a look at this group of marbles.

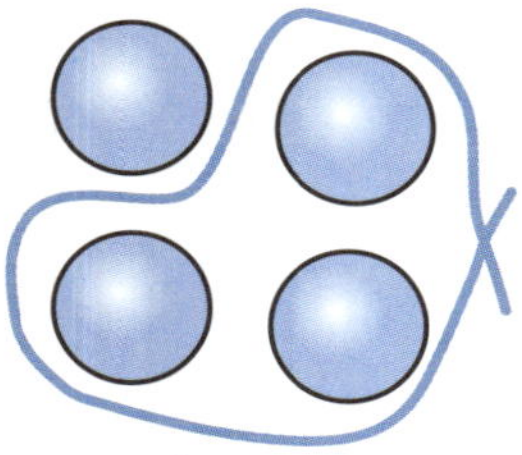

What fraction is circled? Answer $\frac{3}{4}$ or 'three quarters'.

What fraction is not circled? Answer $\frac{1}{4}$ or 'one quarter'.

Try this question.

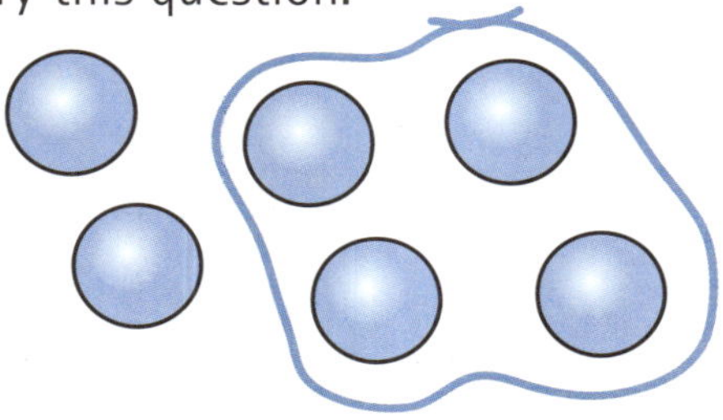

What fraction is circled? Answer

What fraction is not circled? Answer

Equivalent fractions are the same, even though they look different from each other.

Eating $\frac{2}{4}$ of a cake is **the same as** or **equivalent** to eating half of the cake.

Look back at the marbles questions. Using this equivalent fractions chart, can you see what fractions your answers are the same as?

| 1 | | | | | | | |
|---|---|---|---|---|---|---|---|
| $\frac{1}{2}$ | $\frac{1}{2}$ | | | | | | |
| $\frac{1}{3}$ | $\frac{1}{3}$ | $\frac{1}{3}$ | | | | | |
| $\frac{1}{4}$ | $\frac{1}{4}$ | $\frac{1}{4}$ | $\frac{1}{4}$ | | | | |
| $\frac{1}{5}$ | $\frac{1}{5}$ | $\frac{1}{5}$ | $\frac{1}{5}$ | $\frac{1}{5}$ | | | |
| $\frac{1}{6}$ | $\frac{1}{6}$ | $\frac{1}{6}$ | $\frac{1}{6}$ | $\frac{1}{6}$ | $\frac{1}{6}$ | | |
| $\frac{1}{7}$ | $\frac{1}{7}$ | $\frac{1}{7}$ | $\frac{1}{7}$ | $\frac{1}{7}$ | $\frac{1}{7}$ | $\frac{1}{7}$ | |
| $\frac{1}{8}$ | $\frac{1}{8}$ | $\frac{1}{8}$ | $\frac{1}{8}$ | $\frac{1}{8}$ | $\frac{1}{8}$ | $\frac{1}{8}$ | $\frac{1}{8}$ |

Look at one half ($\frac{1}{2}$). Can you see that it is the same as or equivalent to: $\frac{2}{4}$, $\frac{3}{6}$, $\frac{4}{8}$?

Study the chart to find more equivalent fractions. Write two here:

___ is the same as ___     ___ is the same as ___

# Classifying 3D and 2D shapes

## 3D (three dimensional) shapes

3D shapes are solid shapes. When looking at pictures of 3D shapes you have to imagine the bits you can't 'see'.

This picture of a cube shows 3 faces but of course there are actually 6!

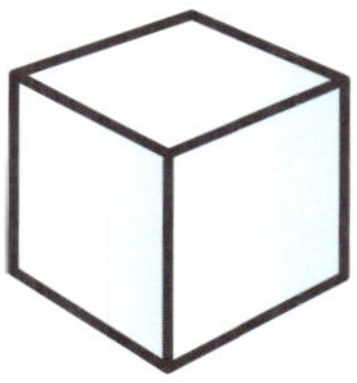

Here are some names of 3D shapes.

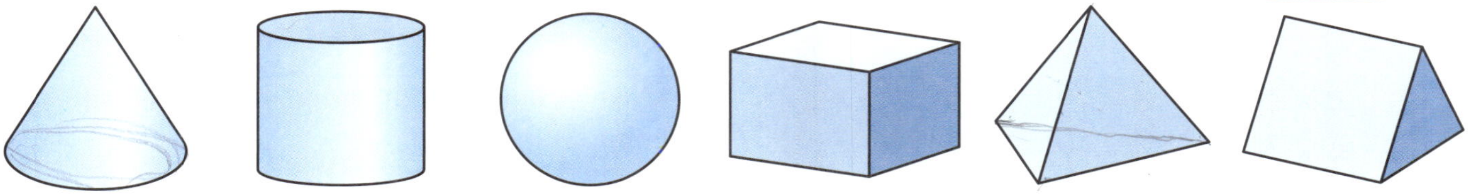

Cone | Cylinder | Sphere | Cuboid | Triangular-based pyramid | Triangular prism

3D shapes are made up of faces, edges and vertices.

- A face is a flat surface of a solid shape.
- An edge is where two faces meet at an angle.
- A vertex is where 3 or more edges meet – a corner.

Complete this chart to help you to understand more about 3D shapes. If you don't have the shapes in front of you, try to picture them in your mind.

| | Cone | Cylinder | Sphere | Cuboid | Triangular-based pyramid | Triangular prism |
|---|---|---|---|---|---|---|
| Number of faces | | | | | | |
| Number of edges | | | | | | |
| Number of vertices | | | | | | |

## 2D (two dimensional) shapes

2D shapes are 'flat shapes'. If they have straight sides they are called polygons. If they have straight sides and all the angles and sides are equal they are called regular polygons.

### Symmetry

A shape is symmetrical (has symmetry) if both sides are the same when a mirror line is drawn. This is also called 'reflective symmetry'.
Take a look:

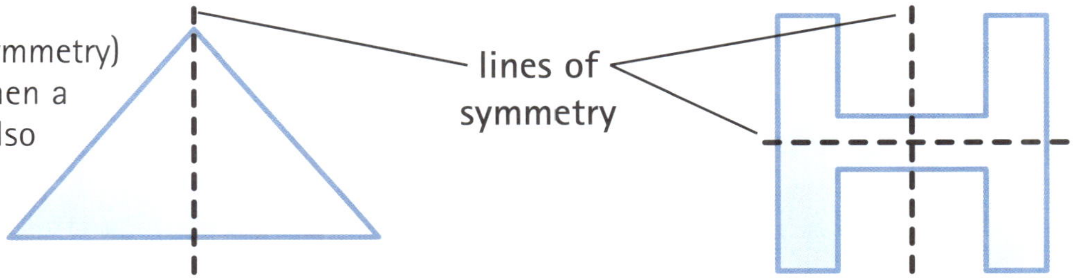

# Tables and lists

Achieved?

In mathematics, information can be presented to you in many different ways. The key to getting a Level 4 is to work out what the graph, table or list is trying to tell you and then answer the questions.

This step-by-step guide will help you to score maximum points on Handling Data questions.

1. Read the question then read it again.
   - There is always a lot of information in these questions. Some you need and some you don't. Always read and think carefully.
2. Look for key words and phrases in the questions.
   - Make sure you understand what you are being asked to find out.
3. Use your finger or a pencil to follow along the rows or down the columns.
   - When you think you've found the information you need, read the question again to double-check.
4. Look back to the question and then read your answer. Does it make sense?
   - If it does, write in your answer. If not go back to Step 1.

## Practice questions

Here is a table about three children in a Year 5 class.

| Like playing with | Jessica | Enya | Thomas |
|---|---|---|---|
| CHAVZ! dolls | ✗ | ✗ | ✓ |
| Toy truck | ✓ | ✓ | ✗ |
| My Little T-Rex | ✓ | ✗ | ✓ |
| The dog | ✗ | ✓ | ✗ |
| Justin from Year 6 | ✓ | ✓ | ✓ |

Read the table. Answer these questions.

1. Who doesn't like my Little T-Rex?

   ______________________

2. Who likes toy trucks?

   ______________________

3. Who doesn't like playing with the dog?

   ______________________

## Tip

Key words and phrases might include:

How many... Who... What is... Where can you find...
Which one... When does... When can... What comes after...

# Bar charts and pictograms

Achieved? ☺ 😐 ☹

When you are reading charts and graphs it is important to have a system so that you can interpret the information accurately. Follow this step-by-step approach and you won't go wrong!

1. Read the information then read it again. — Include the title. What is the graph or chart trying to tell you?
2. Look to see what each axis (or each pictogram) represents.
3. Look at the scale or the numbers going up the side of the graph (the *y* axis). See how much each symbol, or pictogram, is worth. — Do the numbers go up in 1s, 2s, 5s or 10s? If one picture is worth 2 sandwiches, for example, what is half a picture worth?
4. Look at each bar. Read across the scale and work out the amounts. For pictograms, add up the number of symbols for each category. — Make sure you are accurate. Use your finger or a ruler and ALWAYS double-check your final answer.

## Practice questions

Here is a bar chart showing the favourite sandwich fillings in Year 6.

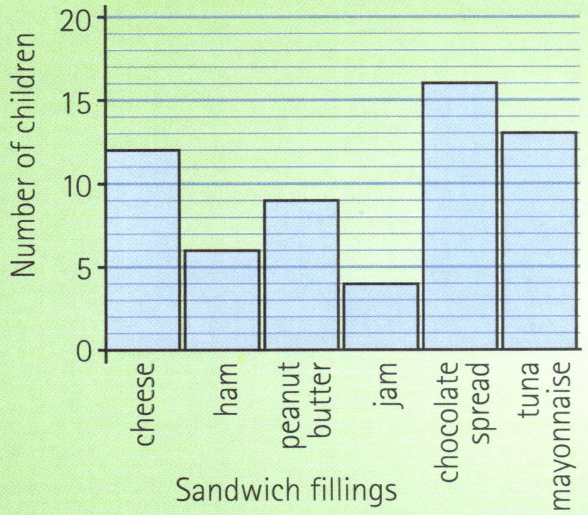


Here is the same information in a pictogram. A pictogram uses symbols to show a group of units.

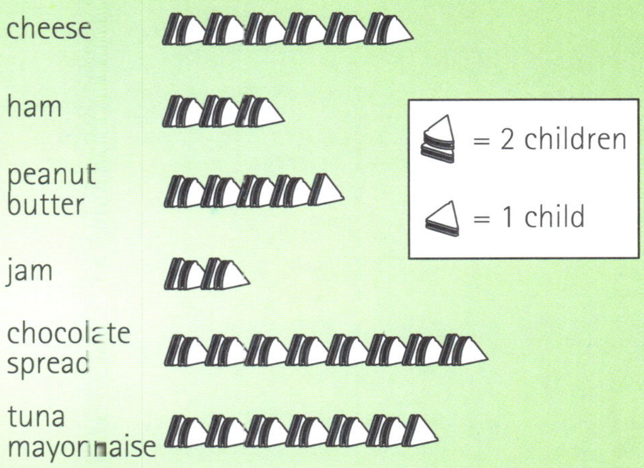


1. Which is the second most popular filling? ______________________
2. How many more children like chocolate spread than peanut butter? ______________________
3. How many children in total like cheese and ham fillings? ______________________

# Short addition

Achieved?

To achieve a Level 4 you will need to add and subtract numbers with digits in the thousands, hundreds, tens and units.

## Let's practise!

What is the total of these numbers?

52, 612, 8, 2127

1. Read the question then read it again.

   "total of"... It's an addition sum.

2. Picture the numbers. Estimate an answer.

   Round the numbers and estimate:
   50 + 600 + 10 + 2100 = 2760

3. Line up the digits in the correct columns.

```
  Th H T U
   2 1 2 7
     6 1 2
       5 2
 +       8
 _________
 _________
```

4. Add up the right hand (units) column. Any total over 9, carry the tens digit to the next column.

```
  Th H T U
   2 1 2 7
     6 1 2
       5 2
 +       8
 _________
         9
 _________
       1
```

5. Repeat with the tens column, remembering to carry any totals over 9. Repeat again with the hundreds and thousands columns.

```
  Th H T U
   2 1 2 7
     6 1 2
       5 2
 +       8
 _________
   2 7 9 9
 _________
       1
```

6. Check your answer against your estimate. Does it look right? If not go back to Step 2.

   Our estimate was 2760. We were very close with 2799!

## Practice questions

1. Find the sum of 523, 24, 7946.
2. Add together 6, 17, 87 and 789.
3. Increase 743 by 1328 and then add 9.
4. Add 3153 to 8826.

# Short subtraction

Achieved?

Now let's try a subtraction question.

## Let's practise!

|  | | |
|---|---|---|
| 1 | Read the question then read it again. | "find the difference between"... It's a subtraction sum. |
| 2 | Picture the numbers. Estimate an answer. | Round the numbers and estimate: 4700 – 500 = 4200 |
| 3 | Line up the digits in the correct columns. | Th H T U<br>4 7 3 4<br>– 4 9 7 |
| 4 | Start with the right hand (units) column and subtract the bottom number from the top. If the bottom number is bigger then 'exchange' a ten from the tens. | Th H T U<br>4 7 ²3̸ ¹4<br>– 4 9 7<br>7 |
| 5 | Repeat with the tens column, remembering to exchange if the bottom number is bigger than the top number. Repeat with the hundreds and then the thousands. | Th H T U<br>4 ⁶7̸ ¹²3̸ ¹4<br>– 4 9 7<br>4 2 3 7 |
| 6 | Check your answer against your estimate. Does it look right? If not go back to Step 2. | Our estimate was 4200. Pretty close to the right answer! That's great. |

## Practice questions

1. How much less than 8468 is 517? ☐
2. Decrease 6624 by 436. ☐
3. What is 8396 minus 436? ☐
4. Take away 1143 from 3668. ☐

# Decimals

Achieved?

Decimals are not whole numbers, e.g. the decimal 3.8 is 'in between' 3 and 4. We say it as '3 point 8'. Let's look at 3.8 on this number line.

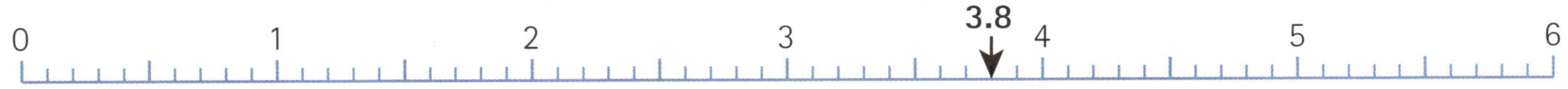


When we add or subtract decimals we need to make sure that we line up the decimal points. Money is written using decimals, e.g. 3.8 would be £3.80.

## Let's practise!

7.92 kg + 7.16 kg + 4.3 kg = ☐

1. Read the question then read it again.
2. Picture the numbers. What do they look like?
   - 7.92 is nearly 8
     7.16 is just over 7
     4.3 is just over 4
3. Study the numbers and think about them! Estimate your answer.
   - 8 + 7 + 4 = 19
     Our answer will be close to 19.
4. Remember the rule! When adding or subtracting decimals, line up the decimal points. Calculate.
   - 7.92
     7.16
     4.30
     19.38
     Add a zero to 4.3 to make them all the same length. Start by adding up the right hand column. Work towards the left.
5. Does your answer look sensible? Check back to your estimate in Step 3.
   - 19.38 is close to our estimate of 19.
6. If your answer looks sensible, write it in the box. If not, go back to Step 2.
   - Yes, our answer of 19.38 kg looks sensible. Always remember to put the units of measurement on your final answer.

## Practice questions

Use the flow chart to work out these additions.

1. 6.34 + 8.77 ☐
2. 67.5 km + 55.8 km ☐
3. £6.67 + £7.26 + £1.99 ☐

Find the difference between these numbers.

4. 19.22 and 27.78 ☐
5. 27.4 and 28.68 ☐
6. 93.29 km and 54.45 km ☐

Let's try a simple question about ordering decimals.

These are the distances jumped in the long jump competition at the school sports day by class 6C.

| | | |
|---|---|---|
| Keeley 3.65 m | Dominic 2.73 m | Harry 2.79 m |
| Jamie 3.75 m | Ellie 3.3 m | Seniz 2.7 m |

Write down the distances in order of size, starting with the furthest jump.

1st ________ 2nd ________ 3rd ________

4th ________ 5th ________ 6th ________

1. Read the question then read it again.
   - Lots of words as well as numbers. Be careful! 'Furthest' means highest number.
2. Write the numbers down underneath each other and line up the decimal points.
   - 3.65
     2.73
     2.79
     3.75
     3.30 Add a zero to 3.3 and 2.7 to
     3.70 make them all the same length.
3. Starting from the top, order the numbers, highest first.
   - Working downwards, which is the highest? 3.75 then 3.65...
4. Continue until all the numbers have been ordered.
   - Now 3.30 is the furthest followed by 2.79. 2.73 is further than 2.70.
5. List them in order and check your answer is sensible. If not, go back to Step 2.
   - 3.75 3.65 3.3 2.79 2.73 2.7
     Work your way down the list. Are they in size order? Yes, so fill in your answer box.

## Practice questions

Put these decimals in order. Start with the smallest number.

1. 8.87, 18.28, 7.87, 1.77, 8.7

   [ ]

2. 2.55 km, 55.2 km, 25.52 km, 5.22 km

   [ ]

3. 9.424, 9.442, 9.242, 9.224, 9.99

   [ ]

4. 0.734, 0.73, 0.773, 0.077

   [ ]

# Multiplying and dividing by 10 and 100

At Level 4 you must be able to multiply and divide whole numbers by 10 and 100.

## Let's practise!

**Write in the missing number.**

$531 \times 10 = \square$

|  | | |
|---|---|---|
| 1 | Read the question then read it again. | 531 × 10 = |
| 2 | Picture the numbers. What do they look like? | 531 lots of 10 or 10 lots of 531. |
| 3 | Remember the rules! | To multiply a whole number by 10 we shuffle the digits one place to the left and add a zero. |
| 4 | Calculate. | 531 × 10. 531 becomes 5310 |
| 5 | Check your answer. | Does 5310 look sensible? Read the answer to yourself. Does it 'fit' the question? |
| 6 | If your answer looks sensible, write it in the box. If not, go back to Step 2. | From Step 2 we know our answer should be in the thousands and we've multiplied by 10 so we only add one zero. Our answer looks correct! |

## KEY FACTS

### MULTIPLICATION

To multiply a whole number by 10 you shuffle the digits one place to the left and add a zero to fill in the space, e.g. $68 \times 10 = 680$

To multiply a whole number by 100 you shuffle the digits two places to the left and add two zeros, e.g. $68 \times 100 = 6800$

### DIVISION

To divide a whole number by 10, you shuffle the digits one place to the right, e.g. $680 \div 10 = 68$

To divide a whole number by 100, you shuffle the digits two places to the right, e.g. $6800 \div 100 = 68$

Let's try another question. This time we will divide a whole number. (Remember: dividing is the opposite of multiplying.)

## Let's practise!

**Write in the missing number.**

**7400 ÷ [ ] = 74**

1. Read the question then read it again.
   - 7400 ÷ [ ] = 74
2. Picture the numbers. What do they look like?
   - What 'fits into' 7400 exactly 74 times?
3. Remember the rules!
   - How many places to the right have the digits been shuffled?
4. Calculate.
   - Shuffle the digits once.
     7400 → 740. We have 740.
     We need to get to 74 so... shuffle the digits again. 740 → 74
     The digits have been moved two places to the right so our answer is 100.
5. Check your answer.
   - Does 100 look sensible? Read the answer to yourself. Does it 'fit' the question?
6. If your answer looks sensible, write it in the box. If not, go back to Step 2.
   - 7400 ÷ 100 = 74
     We can double-check by multiplying 74 by 100 because multiplying is the opposite of dividing. Let's see:
     74 × 100 = 7400. We are correct!

## Practice questions

1. 65 × 10 = [ ]
2. 350 × [ ] = 3500
3. 79 × [ ] = 7900
4. 422 × 100 = [ ]
5. 170 ÷ 10 = [ ]
6. 540 ÷ [ ] = 54
7. 8800 ÷ [ ] = 880
8. 7000 ÷ 100 = [ ]

## Tip

× 10 digits move one place to the left 53 × 10 = 530

× 100 digits move two places to the left 53 × 100 = 5300

# Short multiplication

Achieved?

Short multiplication is two- or three-digit numbers multiplied by a single digit number. Your tables will come in useful when doing calculations like these.

## Let's practise!

What is the product of 482 and 9?

1. Read the question, then read it again.

   "product of"... that's multiplication!

2. Picture the numbers. Estimate an answer.

   Mmm...
   500 × 10...
   Around 5000?

3. Partition the numbers and draw a grid.

| × | 400 | 80 | 2 |
|---|---|---|---|
| 9 | 3600 | 720 | 18 |

4. Multiply the numbers.

| × | 400 | 80 | 2 |
|---|---|---|---|
| 9 | 3600 | 720 | 18 |

5. Add up the answers.

   3600 + 720 + 18 = 4338

6. Check your answers. Does it look right? If not, go back to Step 2.

   What did I estimate the answer was? About 5000.

7. Check your answer against your estimate. Does it look right? If not, go back to Step 2.

   Our answer was fairly close to the estimate. Yes! We were correct.

## Practice questions

1. What is 425 multiplied by 6? ☐
2. What is 713 times 4? ☐
3. Multiply 399 and 5. ☐
4. 362 × 7 = ☐
5. 773 × 9 = ☐
6. 639 × 8 = ☐

# Short division

Achieved?

Short division is dividing a two- or three-digit number by a single digit. Knowing your tables will help you to do these calculations. Division is the opposite or inverse of multiplication, e.g. $4 \times 5 = 20$, so $20 \div 5 = 4$.

## Let's practise!

**What is 274 divided by 8?**

1. Read the question, then read it again. — "divide by" ... that's division!
2. Picture the numbers. What is the task? — How many times does 8 fit into 274?
3. One way of dividing is to think of it as repeated subtraction – the chunking method. What large 'chunks' can we take away? — $274 - 240$ ($30 \times 8$) leaves 34; $34 - 32$ ($4 \times 8$) leaves 2
4. Add up the number of chunks. — $30 + 4 = 34$
5. Are there any remainders? — Yes, we have 2 left over, or 2 remaining.
6. Check your answer. Does it look correct? — Our answer of 34 remainder 2 looks correct.

## Practice questions

1. Divide 288 by 6. ______
2. What is $625 \div 8$? ______
3. Share 891 amongst 3. ______
4. What is 643 divided by 7? ______

# Number patterns

Achieved?

Number patterns or sequences are lists of numbers that follow a pattern. The best way to work out a sequence is to find the 'difference between' the numbers.

## Let's practise!

Fill in the missing numbers and explain the rule in writing.

27, 40, ☐, ☐, 79

1. Read the question then read it again.
   - There are two parts to this question. Don't forget.
2. Picture the numbers.
   - Starting at 27 and going upwards towards 79.
3. Look at the difference between the first two numbers that are next to each other.
   - 27 and 40. The difference is 13.
4. Use the difference you have found and 'test it' on the sequence.
   - 40 + 13 = 53
     53 +13 = 66
     66 + 13 = 79. It fits!
5. If it fits the sequence, then fill in your answer and explain the rule.
   - Fill in the boxes correctly. 53 66
     Explain the rule: 'Add 13 each time.'

## Practice questions

Try filling in the missing numbers in these sequences. Can you explain each rule?

1. –10, –5, ☐, 5, ☐ ____________________
2. 17, ☐, 51, 68, ☐ ____________________
3. ☐, 118, 95, ☐, ☐ ____________________

We are now going to look at three different types of sequence.

## 1 Factors

Factors are numbers that divide exactly into other numbers.

The factors of 12 are: 1, 2, 3, 4, 6 and 12

The factors of 10 are: 1, 2, 5 and 10

### Practice questions

List the factors of:

1. 32
2. 60
3. 42
4. 80

## 2 Prime numbers

A prime number is a number that can **only** be divided by ONE and itself.
The first prime numbers are: 2, 3 and 5
If a number doesn't have any other factors then it is called a PRIME NUMBER.

Can you find all the prime numbers up to 100?

## 3 Multiples

Multiples are numbers made by multiplying two other numbers together.

### ★ Multiples tips

- ★ If a number is a multiple of 2, the last digit will be even. (20, 22, 24, 26...)
- ★ If a number is a multiple of 3, the sum of its digits can be divided by 3. (57 = 5 + 7 = 12 or 114 = 1 + 1 + 4 = 6)
- ★ If a number is a multiple of 4, the last two digits can be divided by 4. (780 or 436 or 916)
- ★ If a number is a multiple of 5, the last digit is a 0 or a 5. (1055, 260, 475)
- ★ If a number is a multiple of 6, it must be an even number and the sum of its digits must be divisible by 3. (1488 = 1 + 4 + 8 + 8 = 21)
- ★ If a number is a multiple of 7, it is a tricky one and you will just have to work it out the long way. 7 is awkward, it doesn't like rules!
- ★ If a number is a multiple of 8, then half the number can be divided by 4! (528 ÷ 2 = 264 ÷ 4 = 66)
- ★ If a number is a multiple of 9, then the sum of its digits is divisible by 9. (378 = 3 + 7 + 8 = 18)
- ★ If a number is a multiple of 10, then the last digit is 0. (290, 1000, 2020)

# Checking your answers

Achieved?

Checking your results should be something you do automatically when you answer a question. It can save you marks in a test and help you to become more accurate with your answers.

Here are five excellent ways you can check the results of your calculations.

## Inverse operations

Remember, adding and subtracting are OPPOSITES. Multiplying and dividing are OPPOSITES. We can use this knowledge to check our answers quickly.

**EXAMPLE**

75 + 95 = 170  Check: 170 − 95 = 75

OR  38 × 6 = 228  Check: 228 ÷ 6 = 38

### Practice questions

1. 524 − 67 = ☐  Check: ☐ + 67 = ☐
2. 160 ÷ 4 = ☐  Check: ☐ × 4 = ☐
3. 7884 − 897 = ☐  Check: ☐ + 897 = ☐
4. 2250 ÷ 50 = ☐  Check: ☐ × 50 = ☐

## Approximate by rounding

Another way to check your answers is to round the numbers in the question up or down to the nearest 10, 100 or 1000. This will give you a simple sum to do first and give you a rough answer.

**EXAMPLE**

297 + 805 is about 300 + 800. Easy! 1100

38 × 19 is about 40 × 20. Easy! 800

You can then check your final answer against your rough answer – they should be fairly close. If not, check your rough answer and then your calculation.

### Practice questions

1. 687 × 11 = ☐  Rough answer ______________________
2. 391 − 108 = ☐  Rough answer ______________________
3. 468 ÷ 18 = ☐  Rough answer ______________________

## Forwards and backwards

When adding several numbers together, try adding them again but backwards.
It doesn't matter what order you add numbers together, the answer will be the same.

Example
11 + 12 + 13 = 36 or 13 + 12 + 11 = 36

Try this sum, starting from the top of the units column.
Now check by starting at the bottom of the units column and continuing. Were you correct?

$$\begin{array}{r} 374 \\ 536 \\ 28 \\ +\ 73 \\ \hline \\ \hline \end{array}$$

## Odds and evens

Knowing about odd and even numbers can help with your checking.

**ADDITION**
- If you add two even numbers, your answer is even.
- If you add two odd numbers, your answer is even.
- If you add one odd and one even number, your answer is odd.

**SUBTRACTION**
- If you find the difference of two even numbers, your answer is even.
- If you find the difference of two odd numbers, your answer is even.
- If you find the difference of one odd and one even number, your answer is odd.

**MULTIPLICATION**
- If you multiply two even numbers, your answer is even.
- If you multiply two odd numbers, your answer is odd.
- If you multiply one odd and one even number, your answer is even.

## Does your answer 'look right'? (Treat your calculator with care!)

It is always worth taking a couple of seconds to redo a calculation to make sure you have pressed the right buttons.
- Think about the question.
- Look at your answer.
- Does it make sense?

**Try this example:**

Billy answers the question 435 × 12 on his calculator.
His calculator displays the answer 48 720.

Billy looks at his answer and knows he is wrong.
He redoes the calculation and gets the answer 5220.

Billy used his knowledge of multiplication by 10 and 100 to help him.
Can you work out what Billy did wrong in his first calculation?

# Recognising proportions of a whole

Achieved?

## Important proportions of whole objects

Simple fractions and percentages can be shown in different ways. Have a look at these shapes. Some fractions have been shaded.

These are all halves...

*Halves* $\frac{1}{2}$ or 50% or 0.5

These are all quarters...

*Quarters* $\frac{1}{4}$ or 25% or 0.25

These are all thirds...

*Thirds* $\frac{1}{3}$ or 33% (approx.)
or 0.33 (approx.)

Let's try this simple question. Remember to use what you have learnt above about proportions to help you find the answers.

120 children in Years 5 and 6 were asked what their favourite animal was.

Can you see the shape of 60 out of 120? This is half of the total.

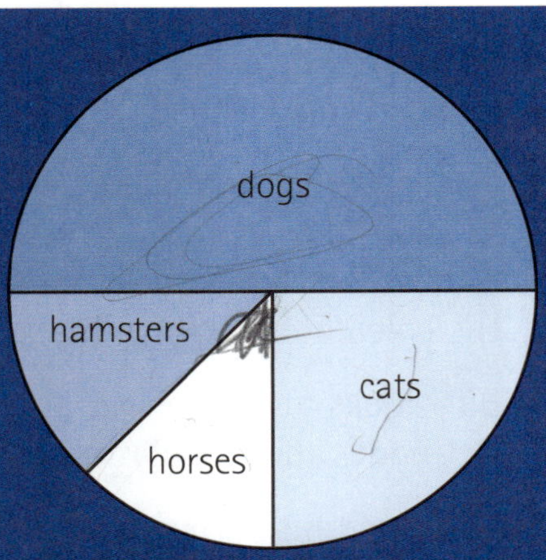


1 Which animal did 60 children choose? dogs

2 How many said the cat was their favourite animal? Can you see the shape of the number of children who chose the cat? It is a quarter.

The answer is $\frac{1}{4}$ of 120 which is 30

## More difficult proportions

These shaded proportions are a little harder – but it's easier if you can recognise them straight away! Try to learn them.

*Three quarters* $\frac{3}{4}$ or 75% or 0.75

These are all three quarters...

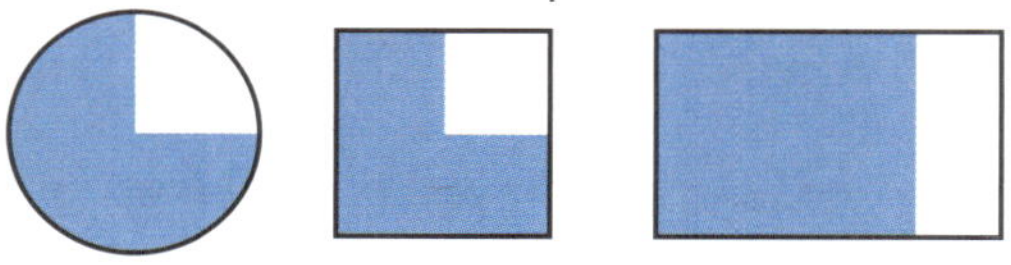

*Two thirds* $\frac{2}{3}$ or 66% (approx.) or 0.66 (approx.)

These are all two thirds...

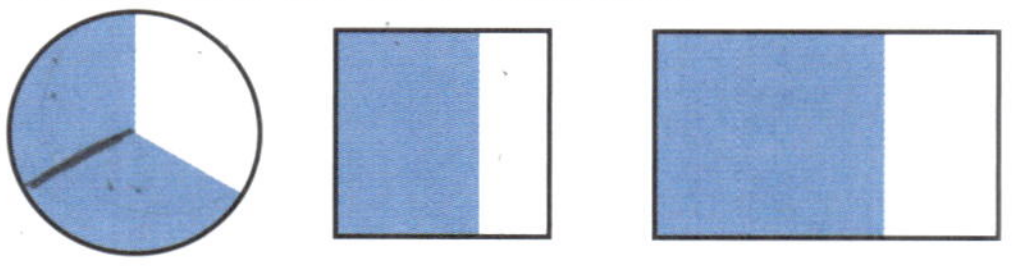

### Practice questions

Practise dividing these circles into equal parts. The first slice in each has been done for you.

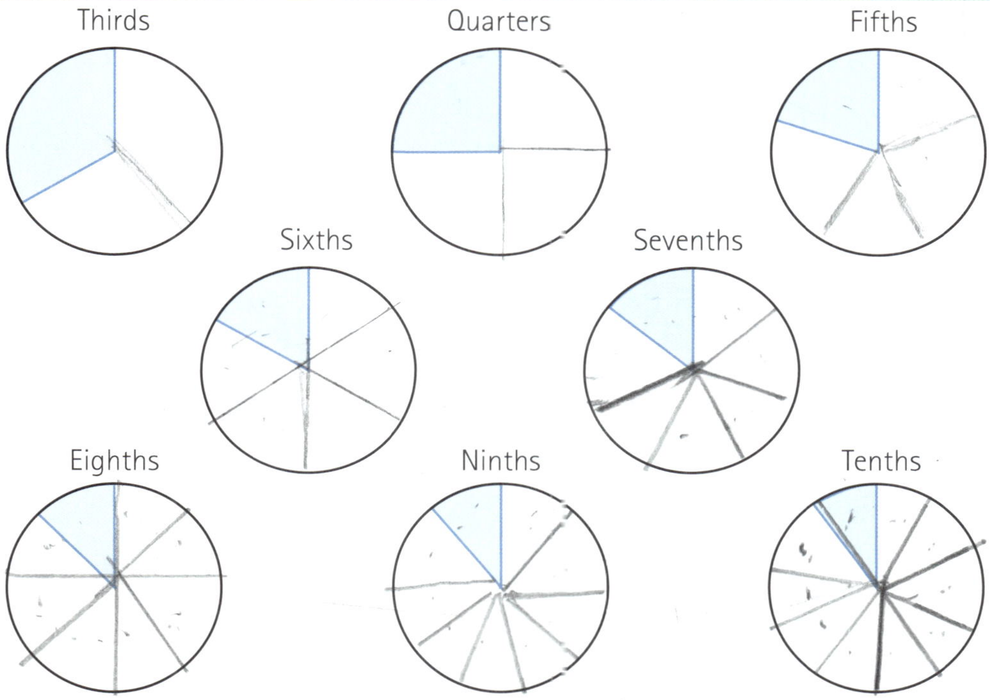


### Tip

Try to picture proportions of objects in your head. Look at the cover of this book. How could you divide it up into equal halves or quarters? Visualise dividing different objects into different proportions of their whole.

# Using coordinates

Achieved? ☺ 😐 ☹

Coordinates are used to identify an exact point on a grid. they are very useful on maps and charts.

Coordinates are written in brackets with a comma in between, e.g. (3, 5).

We always read coordinates ALONG the 'x' axis and up (or down) the 'y' axis.

The 'x' axis is always horizontal and 'y' axis is always vertical.

Have a look at this treasure map.

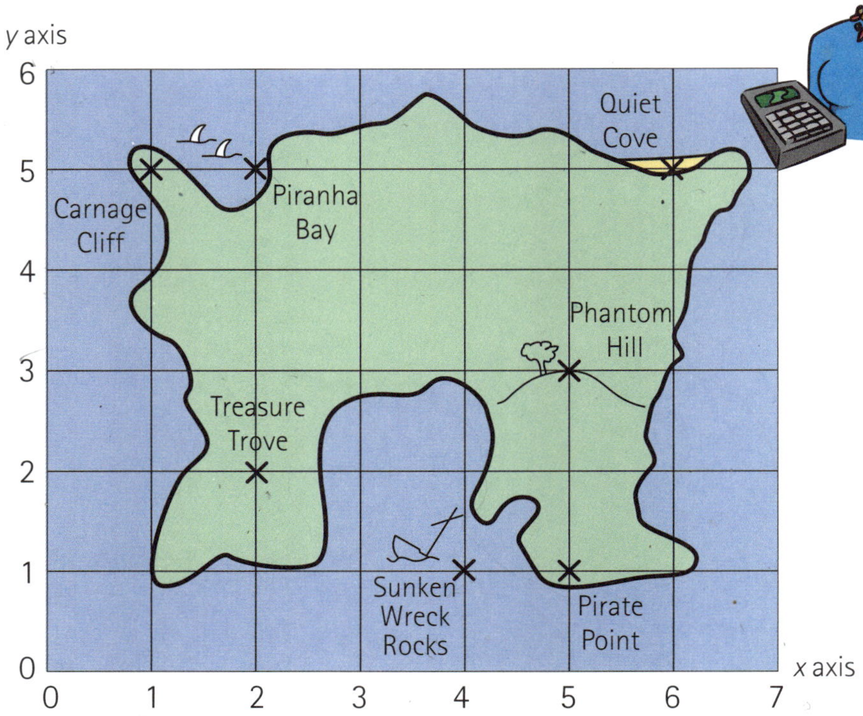


## Practice questions

The coordinates of the buried treasure are (2, 2).
Find this on the map.

**1** What are the coordinates of: Sunken Wreck Rocks? (________, ________)
Piranha Bay? (________, ________)
Quiet Cove? (________, ________)

**2** Where would you be at these points?

(a) (5, 3) ________________________________________

(b) (1, 5) ________________________________________

(c) (5, 1) ________________________________________

### ★ Tip 1

Remember 'x' comes before 'y' in the alphabet.

Always go ALONG the corridor THEN UP the stairs.

### ★ Tip 2

The point (0, 0) is called the origin.

# Finding shapes from a set of coordinates

## Let's practise!

These points are the coordinates of the vertices of a shape.

(2, 1) (4, 1) (5, 3)
(4, 5) (2, 5) (1, 3)

Plot them on the grid. What is the shape?

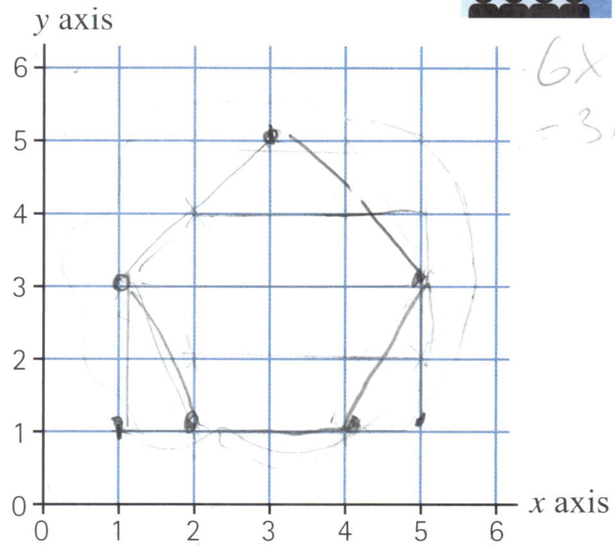


1. Read the question then read it again. — There are words and numbers in this question – read it carefully.
2. Picture the numbers. What do they mean? — The numbers are coordinates.
3. Plot each coordinate in turn. — Go along (*x*) first, then up (*y*). Use your finger first then mark the point with an 'x'.
4. Check each point as you go. Does it look right? — Each time you plot a point, take a look at the shape or pattern that is developing.
5. Join up the points to make the shape. — Lightly draw the shape. Use a ruler and be accurate.
6. Are you happy with the shape? If yes, draw it in. If not, go back to Step 3. — Yes, the shape has 6 sides. It is a regular hexagon.

## Practice questions

On the grid above, can you plot the coordinates of:

1. a rectangle?
2. a pentagon?

Your shapes can overlap each other.

Write the coordinates here:

Rectangle: (1, 1) (5, 1) (1, 3) (5, 3)

Pentagon: (2, 1) (4, 1) (5, 3) (1, 3) (3, 5)

# 3D shapes – making models

Achieved?

To get a Level 4 in mathematics you have to be able to imagine what a 3D shape would look like if it was 'unfolded' – that is, when it is a 'net'.

The net of a solid shape is what it looks like when it has been opened out and laid flat.

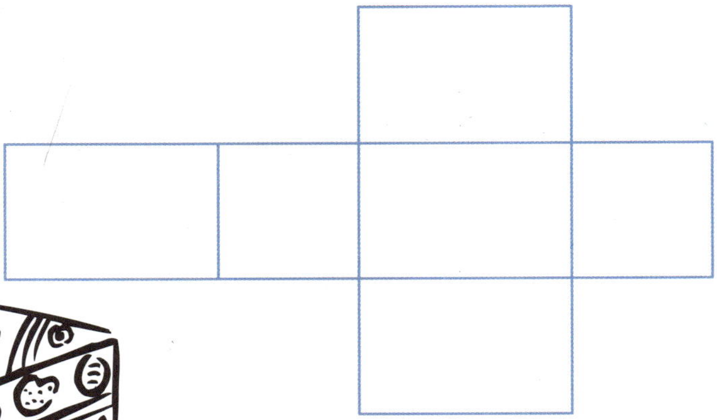

Imagine unfolding a box of chocolates so that the box is just one piece of card.

## Practice questions

Can you link the nets to the 3D shapes? Draw a line to match them up. Try to picture the nets folding themselves up in front of your eyes. Imagination is important in maths you know!

Some shapes, like the cube, have more than one net. Can you see which of these nets would form a cube? Circle them.

# Completing a 3D shape

A popular question is to ask you to visualise 3D shapes that have blocks missing.

## Let's practise!

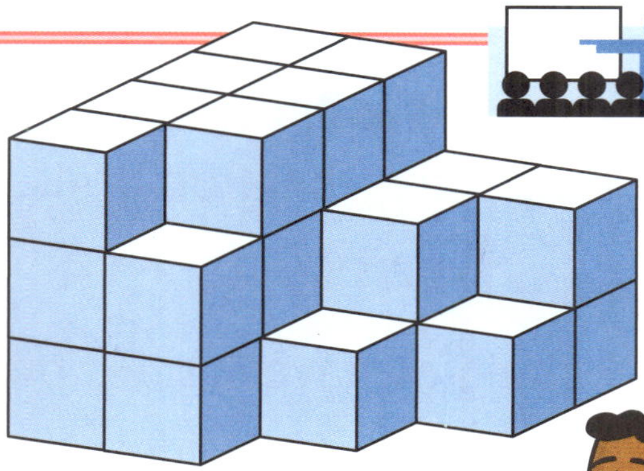

What is the least amount of blocks needed to turn this shape into a cuboid?

1. Read the question then read it again. — What are you being asked to do?
2. Picture the complete shape in your head. — What would it look like? Think about each block. Don't forget to include the blocks you can't see.
3. Work out the dimensions of the shape. — 'Dimensions' means how many blocks long, wide and high it is. This shape is 4 blocks long, 4 wide and 3 high.
4. Calculate the total number of blocks if the shape was complete. — Right, that's $4 \times 4 \times 3 = 48$. 48 blocks would make up the entire cuboid.
5. Calculate how many blocks are in each layer. — There should be 3 layers of 16 blocks because $3 \times 16 = 48$. Cool!
6. Count how many blocks are missing from each layer to get your answer. — Bottom layer: 3 missing.
   Middle layer: 5 missing.
   Top layer: 9 missing.
   $3 + 5 + 9 = 17$ blocks missing.
7. Does your answer look right? If not, go back to Step 1. — Yes it does. We need 17 blocks to turn this shape into a cuboid.

## Practice questions

How many blocks would it take to complete these cuboids?

# 2D shapes

To achieve a Level 4 in mathematics you will need to know all about 2D shapes, including triangles and rectangles. You will also need to know how to draw them on grids.

## Triangles

All triangles have 3 sides but there are different types of triangle!

*Equilateral*

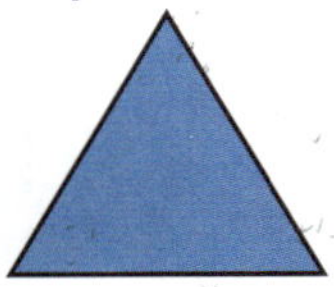

All 3 sides are of equal length.
All 3 angles are equal in size.

*Isoceles*

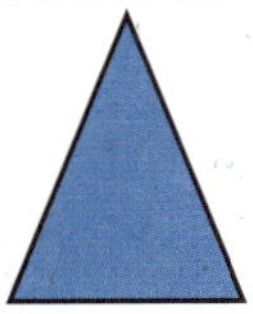

Two sides are equal.
Two angles are equal.

*Scalene*

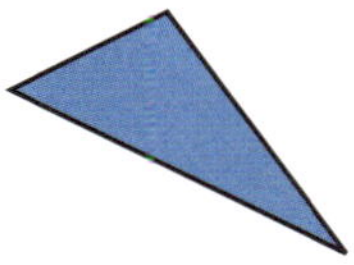

No sides or angles are equal.

*Right-angled triangle*

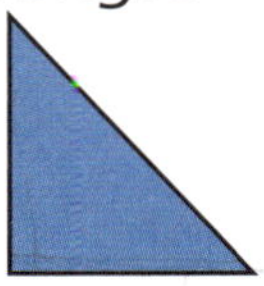

One of the angles is a right angle.

Use these grids to draw 3 examples of each triangle.
Make sure the points (or vertices) of each shape are on the dots.

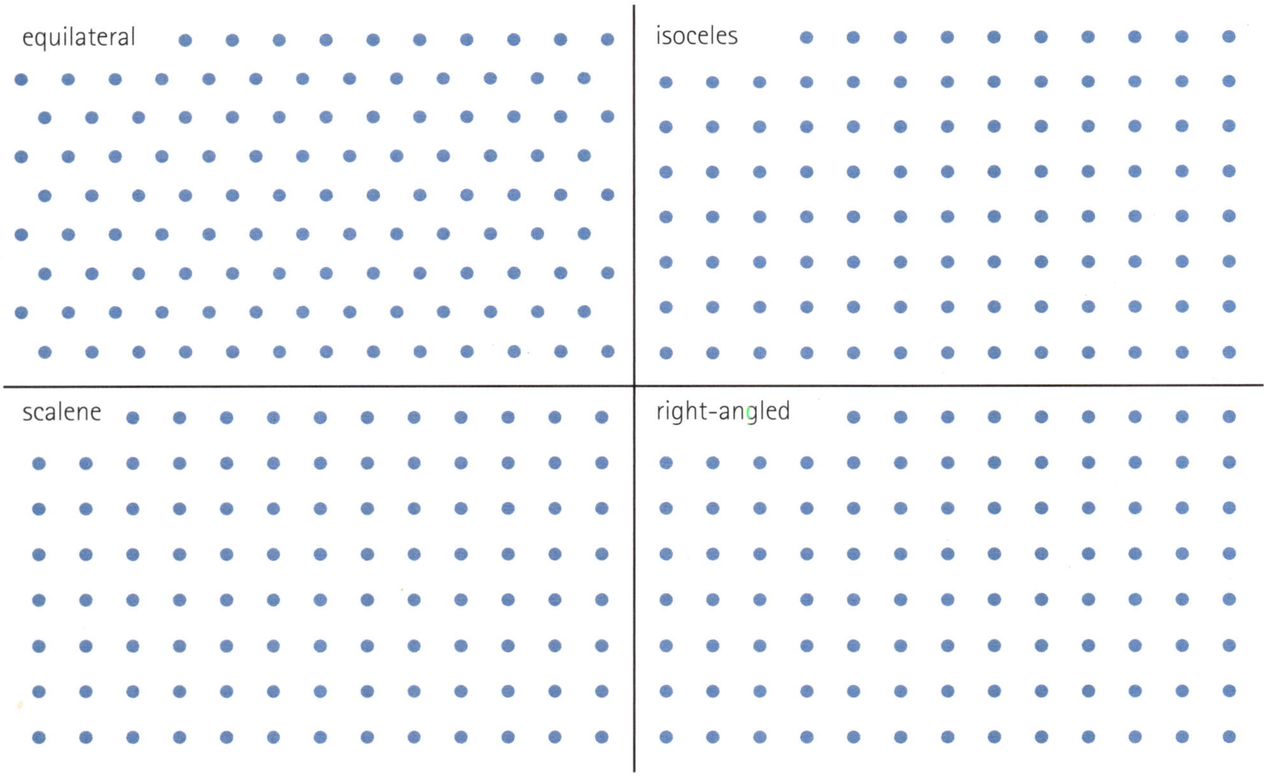


## Tip

Use a sharp pencil and a ruler for this exercise and make sure you have these for your test!

## Rectangles

It is important to learn and remember these properties of a rectangle.

(a) All 4 angles are right angles.

(b) The opposite sides are parallel and equal.

(c) The diagonals bisect each other (blue lines).

(d) There are 2 lines of symmetry (red lines).

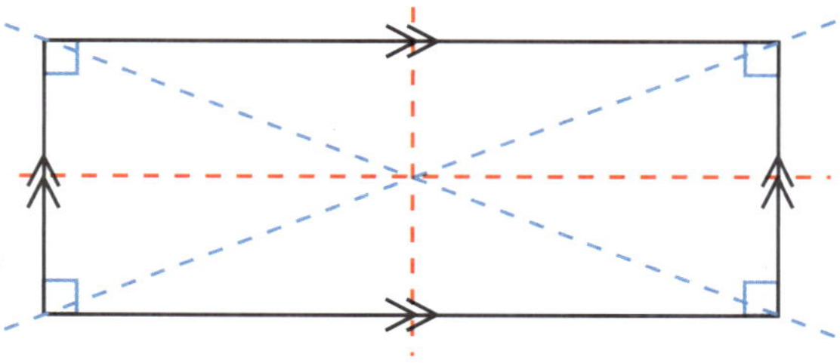

### KEY FACTS

**Parallel** = lines that never meet and are always the same distance from one another. This symbol shows when two lines are parallel ≪ .
**Bisect** = when the lines cross they divide the rectangle into equal parts.
**Square** = a rectangle with four equal sides!

Use this grid to draw 5 rectangles of different sizes.

## Reflections of simple shapes in a mirror line

You should be familiar with reflecting simple shapes – see page 13.
To achieve a Level 4 you need to be able to reflect shapes where either the shape or the mirror line, or both, are at an angle.

For example:

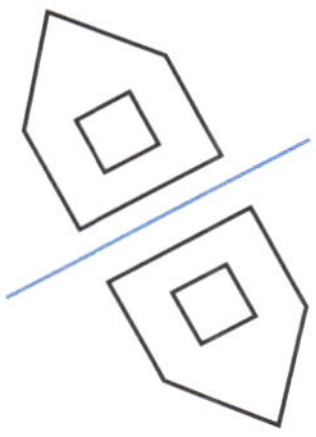

Now try these:

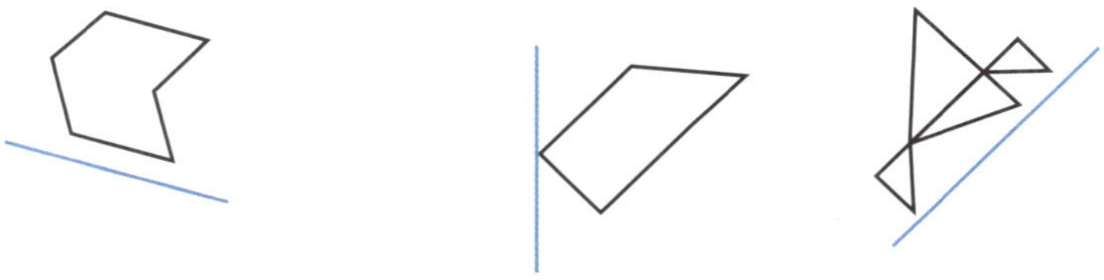

### ★ Tip

When sketching a reflection, picture what the reflection would look like before you draw it.

# Finding the perimeters of simple shapes

Achieved?

The perimeter of a shape is the distance all the way around its edge. This is very easy to work out as long as you remember to follow a step-by-step guide.

## Let's practise!

What is the perimeter of this shape?

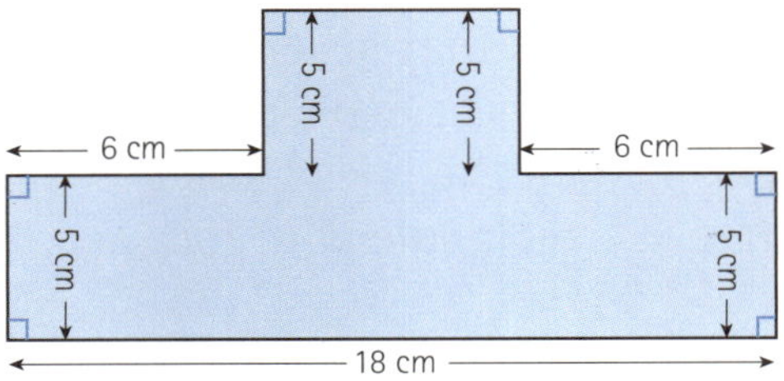


1. Read the question then read it again.
   "Perimeter of". We are being asked to measure the distance around the shape.
2. Choose a side to start from.
   Put a line through it with your pencil. This is the clever part. It helps you to remember where you started.
3. Add up all the lengths that are given in the question.
   5 cm + 6 cm + 5 cm + 18 cm + 5 cm + 6 cm + 5 cm = 50 cm
4. Now work out the length of the side you haven't been given.
   This is the important part. The right angles show you that the distance along the top of the shape must be the same as the distance along the bottom. **Both must be 18 cm.** The **missing** side must be 6 cm because 6 cm + 6 cm + 6 cm = 18 cm.
5. Add the missing length to the total of the lengths you have been given.
   50 cm + 6 cm = 56 cm
6. Does your answer look sensible? If so put it in the box.
   The perimeter of the shape is 56 cm.

### ★ Tip

In this type of question, don't try to measure missing sides with a ruler. The reason they are missing is to test to see if you can work them out from the given lengths.

A perimeter fence goes ALL THE WAY AROUND a building like a prison or a military base.

# Finding areas of shapes by counting

To achieve a Level 4 you will need to find the area of a tricky shape that has been drawn onto squared paper.

## KEY FACTS

The area of a shape is the amount of the surface it covers.

Make sure the units you write are always squared, e.g. $cm^2$ or $m^2$.

## Let's practise!

Each square is 1 square centimetre. What area is shaded?

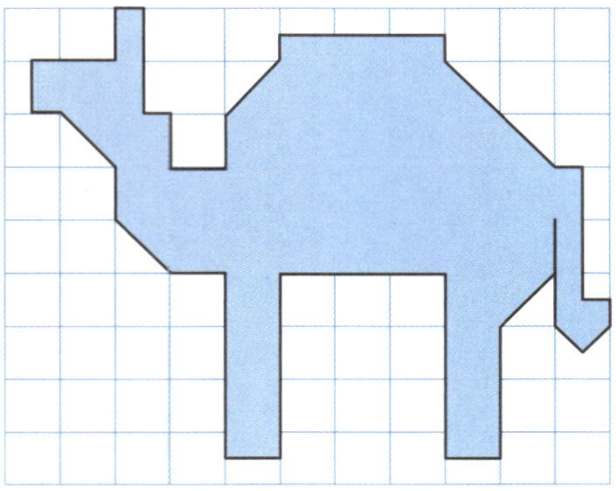

1. Read the question then read it again.
   It is the shaded squares we have to count.
2. Start by counting the whole squares, ticking them off as each is counted.
   Start at the top row and move your finger along to the end counting any **whole** squares. Repeat on the next row. Jot down the total: **31 squares**.
3. Now count the $\frac{3}{4}$ shaded squares.
   OK, start from the top row and work downwards. Jot down the total: **one $\frac{3}{4}$ square.**
4. Now count the $\frac{1}{2}$ shaded squares.
   There are sixteen $\frac{1}{2}$ **squares.**
5. Now count the $\frac{1}{4}$ shaded squares.
   Back to the top again. Work carefully – **there is one $\frac{1}{4}$ square.**
6. Now add together all the fractions.
   One times $\frac{3}{4} = \frac{3}{4}$ ; sixteen halves = 8; one quarter = $\frac{1}{4}$. That makes 9 whole squares.
7. Add the units and square your answer. Does it look sensible?
   31 whole squares + 9 whole squares = 40 $cm^2$.

# Measures

Achieved?

To achieve a Level 4 in mathematics it is important that you know the following things about measures.

(a) Which units of measure to use when measuring length, mass and capacity.

(b) Which instruments to use when measuring length, mass and capacity.

(c) How to read those instruments.

Use the table on this page to learn about the first two!

| | Length of | | | Mass (weight of) | | | Capacity of | | |
|---|---|---|---|---|---|---|---|---|---|
| | Unit | Instrument | Example | Unit | Instrument | Example | Unit | Instrument | Example |
| Small | mm | Ruler | Raisin<br>Sunflower seed | g | Scales | Newspaper<br>Chocolate bar | ml | Teaspoon | Food colouring for cakes |
| Medium | cm | Ruler<br>Metre rule | DVD case<br>Your foot | kg | Bathroom scales | A bag of cement<br>Yourself | cl | Measuring jug | Can of cola<br>Glass of milk |
| Large | m<br>km | Tape measure<br>Metre wheel<br>Tachometer | Distance you can ride a bike | kg<br>tonne | Large scales<br>Weigh bridge | Rhinoceros<br>Tractor | l | Container of of known capacity | Capacity of aquarium<br>Swimming pool |

Here are some questions about the table.

1 Name something you would measure in centimetres.

2 Name something you would measure in centilitres.

3 What instrument would you use to measure the weight of the newspaper?

4 What instrument would you use to measure the length of a sunflower seed?

5 Think of two different things you could measure in:

(a) kg ______ and ______

(b) l ______ and ______

(c) km ______ and ______

Use the table as a guide. Think of some other objects or distances. Where would you 'place' them on the table?

# Reading scales

Achieved?

At Level 4 it is important that you understand how to read instruments of measurement, most of which use scales. The scale will tell you how many of the units of measurement the instrument has measured. The scale might be a dial on a set of scales, lines on the side of a jug or ruler, or decimal numbers in a display.

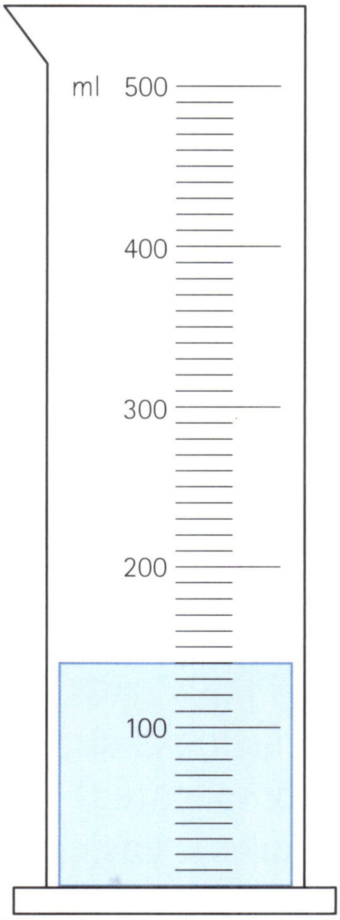


## Let's practise!

350 ml more water is poured into the cylinder. Mark the new level.

1. Read the question then read it again. — We are dealing with measures so we need to be accurate.
2. Picture the numbers. — "350 ml more"
3. Check the unit. What is it: g, l, km? — The measuring cylinder is marked in ml – that's millilitres.
4. If the indicator is on a numbered level, read off that level. — It is between 100 ml and 200 ml.
5. If the indicator is between numbers, then work out what each mark is worth and count forwards or backwards. — OK. The scale goes up by 10 ml each time.
6. Calculate the sum. Mark on the measurement. — 140 ml plus 350 more = 490 ml.

# Grouping data

Frequency charts might have grouped data. This makes the data easier to handle.

Here is a chart showing the number of questions answered correctly by 16 children on a school quiz with 30 questions. We wanted to find out what the most common mark was.

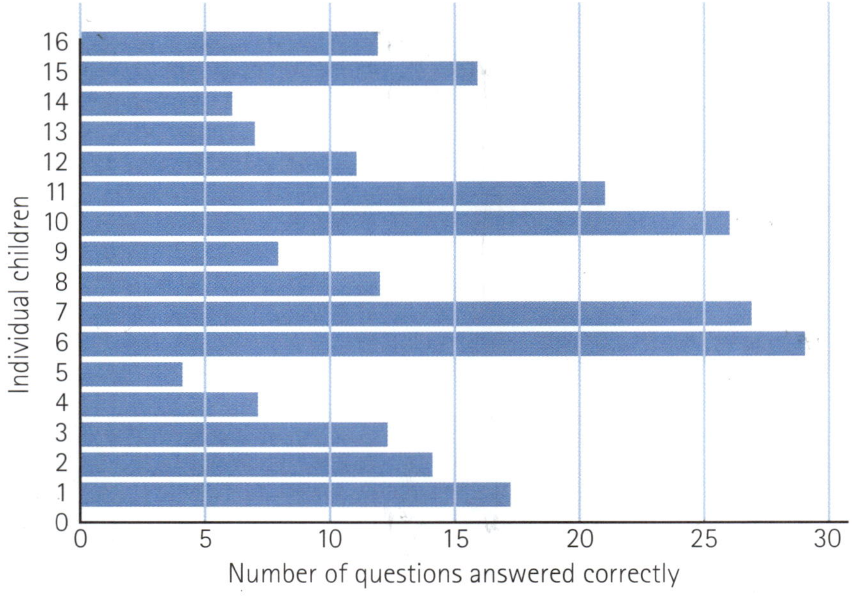


This looks quite complicated! We can make it easier if we group the scores and then compare them. Look at the new chart and answer the questions below.

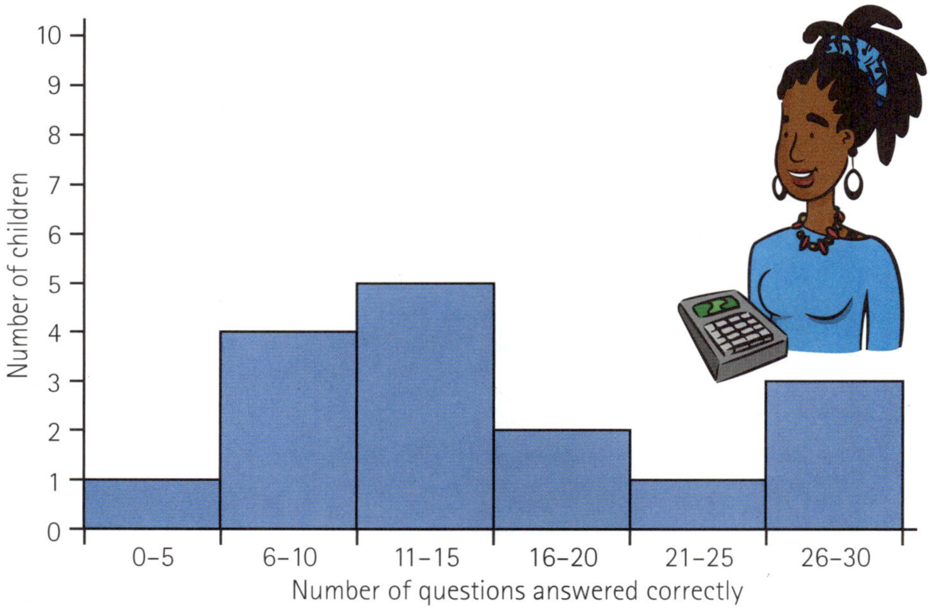


## Questions

1. How many children scored between 16 and 20 marks?
2. How many children scored more than 15 marks?
3. What was the second most common range of scores in the quiz?
4. How many children scored fewer than 21 marks?
5. Look at both of the charts. Did anyone get all the questions right?

## Let's practise!

A week later some children answered the same questions again. Their scores had improved! Here are the results. Can you draw a bar chart and group the data? What was the most common score?

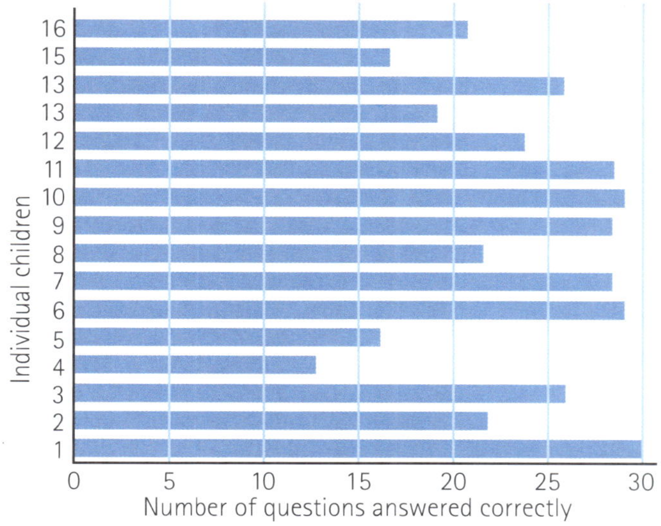

1. Read the question then read it again.
2. Group the data in equal amounts. Mark on your axis.
3. Tally the number for each group of data.
4. Draw in the bars.
5. Check your results. Do they look sensible?

... draw the chart and find the most common score ...

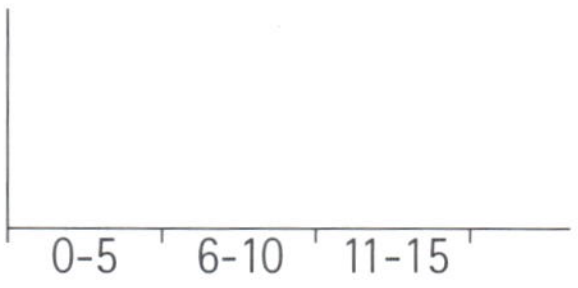


OK. The first group is 0-5. How many children scored 0-5? None, now the next group. None again. Now the 11-15 group. Ah! One. Next the 16-20 group... 3. Next the 21-25 group... 4. Finally the 26-30 group... 8.

The most common score is now between 26 and 30.

Yes, the children scored much higher. This looks right.

### Tip

Think clearly. Work step-by-step.

When handling data, a rough piece of paper can be useful to make notes or tally information.

# Line graphs

A graph with **time** on the ***x* axis** (horizontal) and **numbers** on the ***y* axis** (vertical) is often shown with a line.

Sometimes the graph will show a set of points, joined together by a line. This shows how something is changing over the course of time.

Here is a line graph showing the monthly sales of 'Dudestars™' surfboards over the course of a year.

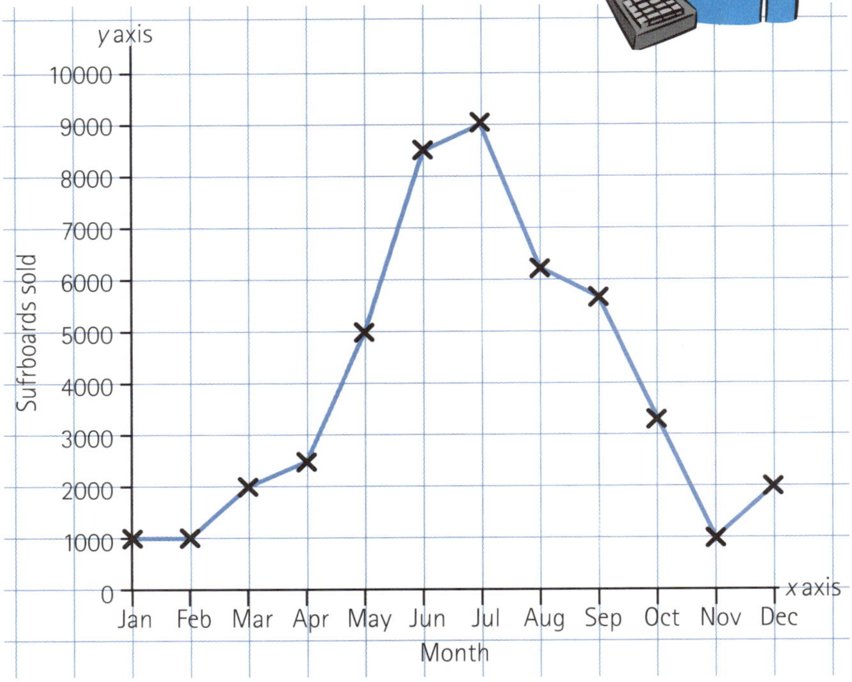


The line in between the points shows a trend or how the sales are changing. It doesn't have any value – only the points themselves have a value.

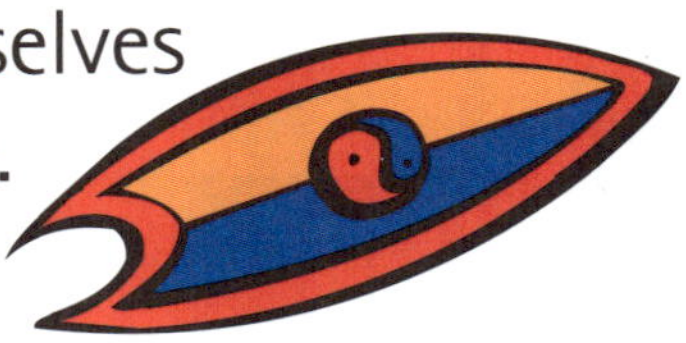

Try answering these questions.

1. Which was the second most successful month? ____________________

   How many surfboards were sold in that month? ____________________

2. Between which two months did the sales of 'Dudestars™' first start to go up?

   ____________________ and ____________________

3. Between which two months did the sales of 'Dudestars™' first start to fall?

   ____________________ and ____________________

4. In which months were more than 6000 surfboards sold? ____________________ and

   ____________________ and ____________________

5. Why do you think there was a rise between November and December? ____________________

## Tip

When reading graphs, go UP from the *x* axis first to meet the line, and then go ACROSS to the *y* axis to read the value.

Chaucer School's foorball team kept a record of their league position each month throughout the season. Can you display this information on a line graph?

| Month | Aug | Sept | Oct | Nov | Dec | Jan | Feb | Mar | Apr | May |
|---|---|---|---|---|---|---|---|---|---|---|
| Position | 12th | 8th | 7th | 5th | 2nd | 2nd | 1st | 3rd | 3rd | 4th |

1. Read the question then read it again. — You need to draw a line graph.
2. Decide which information fits on each axis. — League position (numbers) on the *y* axis and month (time) on the *x* axis.
3. Decide on a scale. — *We need a scale for the league position. The highest is 1st and the lowest is 12th. The range 1-12 seems the most sensible.
4. Plot the points. — This must be accurate. Starting on the *x* axis with August work along to May.
5. Join the points to show the trend. — Does it look like the results in the table?

*You might like to reverse the *y* axis, starting with 12th at the bottom and working up to 1st at the top. This will make it easier to understand when you read it again.

Put the information on the graph using the flow chart to help you. Then answer the questions below.

1. How many months were the team in the top three positions? ____________________
2. Between which two months did their league position improve the most? ____________________ and ____________________
3. How many places did the team drop from February to the end of the season? ________________

## ★ Tip

Always use a sharp pencil when plotting points – it helps you to be more accurate.

# Finding the range

Achieved?

To achieve a Level 4 you will need to find the range of a series of data.

## Let's practise!

This is the price of the same cookery book in four different shops:

£8.99 £14.49 £10.98 £10

What is the range of these prices?

1. Read the question then read it again.
2. Think about the question. — The range is the difference between the **lowest** and **highest** value.
3. Picture the numbers. — Put them in order, lowest first: £8.99, £10, £10.98 and £14.49.
4. Study the numbers. — The most expensive is £14.49. The cheapest is £8.99. What is the difference between these costs?
5. Calculate your answer. — £14.49 – £8.99 = £5.50
6. If your answer looks sensible, write it in the box. — If not, go back to Step 3 and try again.

## Practice question

Rising Stars Bookshop sells lots of books. What was the range of books sold for the second half of 2002?

2002

| | | | | | |
|---|---|---|---|---|---|
| July | 16 700 | August | 23 414 | September | 11 103 |
| October | 25 777 | November | 28 993 | December | 30 444 |

### ★ Tip

Scan the list and mark the lowest number.

### ★ Tip

Check through the list to see if it really is the lowest. Repeat for the highest number.

# Finding the mode

Achieved?

Your test might also contain questions on mode.

## Let's practise!

These are the ages of the Bright Stars football team.

18 22 23 29 22 18 29 23 22 23 22

What is the mode of these ages?

1. Read the question then read it again.
2. Think about the question. — The mode is another name for the most common value.
3. Picture the numbers. — Make sets of the same number.

| | | | |
|---|---|---|---|
| 18 | 22 | 23 | 29 |
| 18 | 22 | 23 | 29 |
| | 22 | 23 | |
| | 22 | | |

4. Double-check. — Make sure you haven't missed any numbers.
5. Decide on your answer. — 22 occurs most often. 22 is the mode.
6. If your answer looks sensible, write it in the box. — If not, go back to Step 3 and try again.

## Practice question

The children in Class 4 have different numbers of brothers and sisters. What is the mode of the number of siblings?

2 4 1 0 0 2 1 3 2 3 4

### Tip 1

Remember:

**Mode** is the **M**ost **C**ommon **V**alue

**Modal** means **Mode**

### Tip 2

Always write out the numbers again and sort them.

Tick off each number so you know you haven't missed any of them. **This is IMPORTANT!**

# Using simple formulae

Achieved?

A formula is a way of explaining a rule. To achieve a Level 4 you need to be able to explain a given rule in writing.

## Let's practise!

Explain how to find the number of months in any number of years.

| Step | | |
|---|---|---|
| 1 | Read the question then read it again. | It is all words. You have to work out any numbers involved. |
| 2 | Picture the numbers and the words. | The key word here is 'explain'. You also need to show that there are 12 months in a year. |
| 3 | Talk through the rule in your head. | To find the number of months in any number of years, you must multiply the number of years by 12... |
| 4 | Test your rule. Does it work? If not, go back to Step 1. | Make your test simple to avoid mistakes, e.g. 4 years = 4 × 12 = 48 months. |
| 5 | Write your rule as simply as possible. | 'The number of months in any number of years = the number of years multiplied by 12.' |
| 6 | Check your answer. Does it make sense? | Read it through to yourself. Does your formula work? |

### Tip 1

Rehearse your sentences in your head before you write them.
When you have written them, read them back to yourself. Have you thought clearly?
Have you said what you wanted to say?

### Tip 2

The '=' sign means 'the same as'

e.g. 2 + 2 = 4 — 2 + 2 is the same as 4

10 – 5 = 8 – 3 — 10 – 5 is the same as 8 – 3

A simple formula is often used to find out the total cost of items bought. In words this formula can be written:

**"The total cost is the cost for one item multiplied by the number of those items bought."**

In letter formulae this could be written as: $T = P \times N$

$T$ = total cost $P$ = cost of each item $N$ = number of items bought

## Practice questions

Use the $T = P \times N$ formula to work out these questions.

1. What is the value of $T$ if $N = 2$ and $P = £4.50$?
2. What is the value of $N$ if $T = £20$ and $P = £4$?
3. What is the value of $P$ if $T = £24$ and $N = 6$?

## Example question

Andrea and Jamie are playing a number game. Jamie gives Andrea a number, which she changes using a rule:

*"I take Jamie's number and multiply it by 7, then subtract 2."*

Write a formula to show the process Andrea goes through to get to her answer.

Use J for Jamie's number and A for Andrea's answer.

$A = (J \times 7) - 2$

## Practice questions

Now Andrea changes the rule:

*"I take Jamie's number and multiply it by 9 then add 3."*

Write a formula to show the process Andrea goes through to get to her answer. Use J for Jamie's number and A for Andrea's answer.

A =

## Tip

If a number and a letter are next to each other, e.g. 4N, it means they are multiplied. Why is the × (multiply) symbol left out? Because it could get confused with the letter x!

# Using and applying mathematics

Achieved?

## Introduction

The reason for learning all the different mathematical skills (multiplying, dividing, measuring, estimating and so on) is so you can use them to solve mathematical problems.

Imagine learning all the shots in tennis, like the serve, the volley, the backhand and forehand, but never actually getting to play a game! Only by using your shots in a match will you learn to be a tennis player. Likewise, only by using your mathematical skills will you learn to be a mathematician!

The flow chart opposite is designed to guide you when tackling a maths problem. It will help organise your thinking, but it won't tell you the answer – that's for you to work out for yourself.

The next few pages contain problems for you to solve. Work through the examples first and then have a go at the practice questions using the flow chart approach.

Good luck!

## Problem solving

### NUMBER

These questions are all about your number skills. You must use them in the right way though!

### MEASURES

These questions are all about real situations: going on a journey, the amount of milk a family drinks in a week and so on.

### SHAPE AND SPACE

These questions all require you to use your knowledge about shapes, both 2D and 3D.

### HANDLING DATA

These questions often ask you to find out information from a table or chart. They will also ask you to explain how you found out the answer!

# The Problem Solving Flow Chart

1. **Read the question then read it again.**
   Read through the question slowly. Twice. Let the words and numbers 'sink in'.

2. **Picture the words and numbers. What do they mean?**
   What does this problem mean to you? You could draw a picture or diagram to help you. You could write it in your own words.

3. **Highlight key words and phrases.**
   Look for mathematical phrases like 'find the difference between', and 'what is the product of'. Work out what is important information and what isn't.

4. **Can you estimate an answer?**
   This will depend on the question. Estimate using the information you have. Don't guess wildly.

5. **What calculations do you need to do?**
   Work out what needs to be added, subtracted, multiplied and divided. Sometimes you may need to perform more than one function. Write the calculations down but don't do them yet.

6. **What is the answer to your calculations? Show how you got your answer.**
   Now calculate if you need to. Estimate first. Write down your method – it shows how well you are thinking. Check your answer.

7. **What is the answer to the original problem? Write it in full sentences.**
   Does your answer match what you have been asked to do? Don't just give one word or number answers (e.g. 12). Write it in a clear sentence (e.g. The number that Sofie was thinking of was 12.)

8. **Is your answer a sensible one?**
   Does your answer make sense? Is it realistic? If the problem is a real-life problem, have you got a real-life answer?

## ★ Tips

- Remember your 'checking the answer' skills.
- Think clearly and write clearly.
- Present your work so it shows what you have done.
- Work step-by-step.
- Make a problem easier (e.g. Find 24 lots of 6. Try finding 4 lots first then 20 lots.)
- Take a reasonable guess at what you think might happen.
- Think HOW you are working. Change your method if something isn't working.
- Look for patterns in your maths.

# Solving number problems

Achieved? ☺ 😐 ☹

Let's try a simple number problem.

The numbers in row 2 of this triangle of snooker balls have been found from the two numbers directly above them using a rule. Fill in the missing numbers and write the rule.

Rule:

1. Read the question then read it again.
   There are two things to do to complete this question – "find the missing numbers" and "write the rule".

2. Picture the words and numbers. What do they mean?
   How are these numbers 'linked'? When we have worked it out, we need to *explain* how.

3. Highlight key words and phrases.
   "numbers in row 2", "found from the two numbers directly above".

4. Can you estimate an answer?
   No, because the answer is not immediately obvious.

5. What calculations do you need to do?
   Work step-by-step. Start with 84 and 72. What do we have to do to get 78… Add? Subtract?

6. What is the answer to your calculations? Show how you got your answer.
   84 + 72 = 156 and 84 – 72 = 12… Look at our answers. Can we see any 'link' with 78? Yes! 78 is half of 156 or double 78 is 156. Have we found the rule?

7. What is the answer to the original problem? Write it in full sentences.
   The rule is add the two numbers together and divide the total by two. We can also fill in the missing numbers.
   (78 + 80) ÷ 2 = 79; (80 + 66) ÷ 2 = 73;
   (79 + 73) ÷ 2 = 76

8. Is your answer a sensible one?
   Yes, we've applied our rule throughout the triangle and it works!

## Practice questions

Use the flow chart to help you to answer this number problem 'story'. Show your method for each calculation you do.

Crime boss 'Eadcase 'Arry suspects his two top henchmen, Baz and Gaz, of being thieves. As if! 'Eadcase decides to find out by setting them a little test – trial by shopping! If they're so much as a penny short, he'll show them how he got his nickname... 'Eadcase tells Baz and Gaz that their hideout is looking a bit scruffy and that it needs a good makeover. He gives them £250 each to spend in ODEA – the home improvement store. However, 'Eadcase wants all receipts and any change that's left over. Any thieving and he'll know about it! This is how Baz and Gaz spend the money...

**1** Baz gave the cashier £250 and got £88.01 change. How much were the candles?

Baz's Receipt
Lounge furnishings
Light oak coffee table £95
Sheepskin rug £32
Soft-light lamp £16.99
Candles

Show your method.

**2** Gaz gave the cashier £250 and got £38.01 change. How much was the fondue set?

Gaz's Receipt
Kitchen additions
Juicer £95
Seven-piece saucepan set £62
Butchers' block £29.99
Fondue set

Show your method.

**3** Baz and Gaz pay £25 to have the goods delivered and £17.60 for a taxi back to the hideout. They give 'Eadcase 'Arry his £83.32 change and receipts... Explain how this story ends, giving your reasons!

# Solving measures problems

Let's try a simple measures problem.

Here is a list of ingredients for banana mousse.
It feeds 4 people.

1.2 kg of bananas — 6 eggs
300 ml milk — 4 tablespoons caster sugar

Gordon wants to prepare banana mousse for 6 people. Can you change the amount of each ingredient so he makes enough mousse? **Show your method:**

1. Read the question then read it again.
   Change the amounts of four ingredients...

2. Picture the words and numbers. What do they mean?
   We could draw each item.
   4 × 300 g = 1.2 kg.

3. Highlight key words and phrases.
   Change the amounts from 4 to 6. Ah! That's an increase of 'half as much again' or 50%.

4. Can you estimate an answer?
   We can easily work out the number of eggs and the amount of sugar. Gordon now needs 6 eggs plus half as many again, so that's 9 eggs, and 6 tablespoons (4 + 2) of sugar. We can estimate an answer of 1.5 kg of bananas and 500 ml of milk.

5. What calculations do you need to do?
   (50% of 1.2 kg) + 1.2 kg
   (50% of 300 ml) + 300 ml.

6. What is the answer to your calculations. Show how you got your answer.
   50% of 1.2 kg = 600 g.
   1200 g + 600 g = 1800 g or 1.8 kg.
   50% of 300 ml = 150 ml
   300 ml + 150 ml = 450 ml

7. What is the answer to the original problem? Write it in full sentences.
   Check answers against our estimate. Gordon would need 1.8 kg of bananas, 450 ml of milk, 9 eggs and 6 tablespoons of sugar.

8. Is your answer a sensible one?
   Yes, these look sensible amounts for 6 banana mousse!

## Practice questions

Use the flow chart to help you answer these questions about measure.
The fun-fair is in town!

**1** Mystery Rose has made 400 litres of her special hedgerow punch for the visitors to sample. One cup of punch is 250 ml. How many cups of punch can Mystery Rose sell?

Show your method.

**2** The Grand Canyon rollercoaster is 328 m long. If a ride on the rollercoaster is 6 laps long, how far does the rider travel? Give your answer in metres, and then kilometres.

Show your method.

**3** The strongman Billy Biceps is demonstrating his great strength. He puts 4 children into a bathtub and lifts them all above his head! The children weigh 46.5 kg, 39 kg, 52.8 kg and 33.2 kg. The bathtub weighs 30 kg. How much does Billy Biceps manage to lift altogether.

Show your method.

**4** The Tunnel of Love water ride has sprung 4 leaks. The ride contains 10 000 litres of water. Each leak loses 482 litres. How much water is left for the ride to operate?

Show your method.

**5** A customer on the ferris wheel travels 1344 m during the course of the ride. One revolution of the wheel is 56 m. How many times does the wheel revolve for one ride?

Show your method.

**6** The Tubbs, a hungry family of 6, eat toffee apples and popcorn during their visit to the fair. Each of the Tubbs eats 350 g of toffee apples and 475 g of popcorn. How many kilograms of food do the family Tubbs consume?

Show your method.

# Solving shape and space problems

Achieved?

Let's try a simple shape and space problem.

How many rectangles can you see in this shape?

Show your method:

1. Read the question then read it again.
   - Study the words. Study the shape. Think past 'the obvious'.
2. Picture the words and numbers. What do they mean?
   - It would help to sketch the shape on some rough paper. Think how you could work in a logical step-by-step way.
3. Highlight key words and phrases.
   - "How many". We are going to need a total number of rectangles to be correct. Saying 'lots' won't be good enough!
4. Can you estimate an answer?
   - We can see 9 inside the big one straight away. That's 10. Let's say double that. 20?
5. What calculations do you need to do?
   - Work in a logical way using a table. How many 1-unit rectangles are there? How many 2-unit rectangles are there? And so on...
6. What is the answer to your calculations? Show how you got your answer.

| Number of units | 1 | 2 | 3 | 4 | 5 | 6 | 7 | 8 | 9 | 10 | Total |
|---|---|---|---|---|---|---|---|---|---|---|---|
| Number of rectangles | 9 | 12 | 6 | 4 | 0 | 4 | 0 | 0 | 1 | 0 | 36 |

7. What is the answer to the original problem? Write it in full sentences.
   - We can see 36 rectangles in this shape.
8. Is your answer a sensible one?
   - It looks sensible because we worked in a step-by-step way. Our estimate was quite a long way out, but a logical approach has given us the correct answer.

## Practice questions

Use the flow chart to help you to answer these questions about shape and space.

**1** How many equilateral triangles can you see in this diagram?

Show your method.

**2** How many squares can you count?

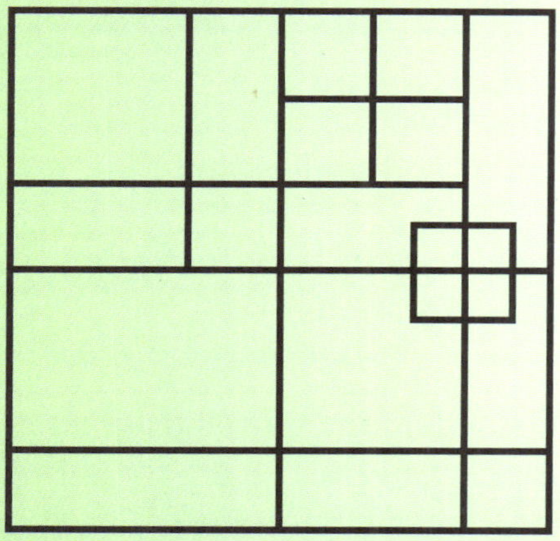

Show your method.

**3** Imagine a dice and an open box that is just big enough to hold it.

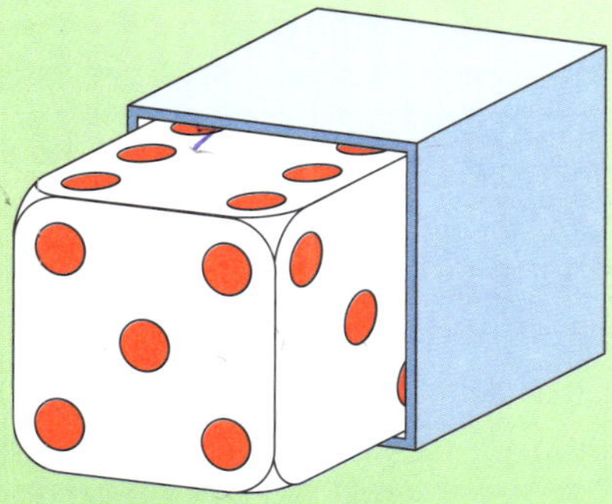

How many ways can you fit the dice into the open box?

Show your method.

# Solving data handling problems

Let's try a simple data handling problem.

Theo has carried out a survey of some popular computer games. Find *Gran Theft Skateboard, HALO 5* and *Wrestling Fest* in the Carroll diagram below. Write them in the correct place on the Venn diagram.

| | Suitable for ages 12 and under | Not suitable for ages 12 and under |
|---|---|---|
| 1 player only | Gran Theft Skateboard<br>Speed Racer 2 | Zombie Hunter<br>Horror-shocker |
| 2 or more players | Wrestling Fest | Car-jacker<br>HALO 5 |

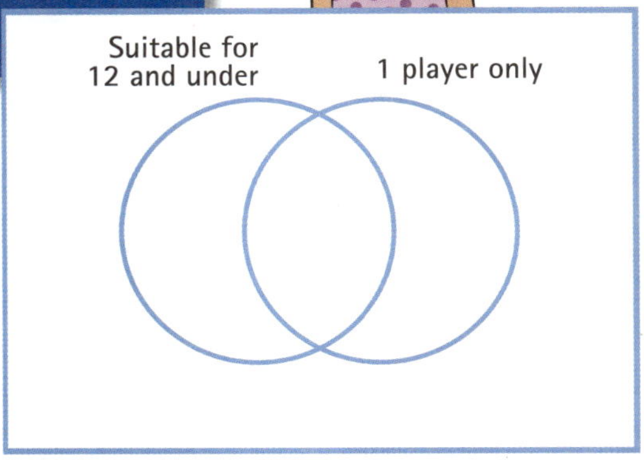


1. Read the question then read it again.
   There are two different diagrams to look at and understand.
2. Picture the words and numbers. What do they mean?
   We need to transfer information from one diagram to another.
3. Highlight key words and phrases.
   Understanding the Carroll diagram is important. Car-jacker and HALO 5 are for 2 or more players and NOT suitable for ages 12 and under.
4. Can you estimate an answer?
   No, it would be a wild guess.
5. What calculations do you need to do?
   No calculations here. We need to put three games in the correct positions on the Venn diagram.
6. What is the answer to your calculations? Show how you got your answer.
   *Wrestling Fest* is for ages 12 and under but needs 2 or more players, so it goes in the left hand circle. *Gran Theft Skateboard* is for 12 and under AND 1 player only, so it goes where the 2 circles meet., *HALO 5* doesn't fit in either category so goes outside both circles.
7. What is the answer to the original problem? Write it in full sentences.
   Now we can fill in the Venn diagram with the three games in the correct places.
8. Is your answer a sensible one?
   After double-checking what we have written and where, it is a sensible answer.

# Practice questions

Use the flow chart help you to answer these data handling questions.

**1**

I am trying to find a number. It is a multiple of 7. It is an even number. It is less than 25. What is the number?

Complete this table to help you find the answer.

| Multiples of 7 less than 25 | Even numbers less than 25 |
| --- | --- |
| | |

Show your method.

**2**

My number is a square number. It has two digits but is less than 50. It is divisible by 3. What is my number?

*Clue: Try using a table like the one in question 1.*

Show your method.

**3**

Six villages are joined together by a bus route. The bus goes from A and back to A.

It visits each of the other towns once.
How many different bus routes are there?

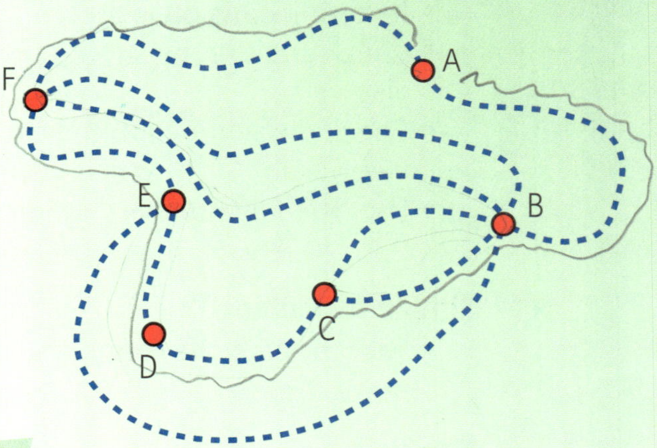


Show your method.

**4**

Isobel, Ollie, William, Sam and Kay all meet at school. Each child shakes hands with every other child. How many handshakes are there altogether? Use a diagram to help you.
Show your method.

# KEY FACTS

## The Number System and Calculations

### Place value

- Each number is made up from digits. Where these digits are in a number gives that number its value.

| | Hundreds | Tens | Units | |
|---|---|---|---|---|
| 784 | 7 | 8 | 4 | = 700 + 80 + 4 |

### Multiplying decimals by 10, 100 and 1000

- Shuffle numbers to the left.
- Shuffle numbers to the left once when × 10, twice when × 100 and three times when × 1000.

### Dividing decimals by 10, 100 and 1000

- Shuffle numbers to the right.
- Shuffle numbers to the right once when ÷ by 10, twice when ÷ by 100, and three times when ÷ by 1000.

### Negative numbers

- Integers are just whole numbers.
- When counting from negative up to positive or positive down to negative, **remember to count 0!**
- When counting on a number line, count to the right when adding, count to the left when subtracting.

### Decimals to two places

- When rounding, remember 5 is up!
  6.785 = 6.79

### Fractions

- A fraction is 'part of a whole number'.

| | | |
|---|---|---|
| 1 | the numerator | The numerator tells you how many equal parts there are. |
| 2 | the denominator | The denominator tells you the number of equal parts the whole nmber is divided into. |

### Reducing a fraction to its simplest form

- To reduce a fraction to its simplest form, find a common factor which you can divide into the numerator and the denominator.
  For example, $\frac{3}{9} \frac{\div 3}{\div 3} = \frac{1}{3}$

### Calculating a fraction or percentage

- Remember as many percentage/fraction equivalents as you can:

$50\% = \frac{1}{2}$   $25\% = \frac{1}{4}$   $75\% = \frac{3}{4}$

$33\% =$ nearly $\frac{1}{3}$   $66\% =$ nearly $\frac{2}{3}$

### Multiplication and division (with decimal points)

- × and ÷ are opposites.
- Always estimate first. It will help you to get the decimal point in the right place if one is needed.

### Checking your answers

- Inverse means opposite!
- Check addition by subtraction – and vice versa.
- Check division by multiplication – and vice versa.
- Use 'friendly numbers' when estimating: 2, 5, 10, etc.

### Simple formulae

- Talk through the formula in your head. It will make it easier.

### Brackets

- Always do brackets in equations first.

### Coordinates

- Always read ALONG ($x$ axis) and then UP ($y$ axis).
- Always write ($x$) before ($y$) – ($x$, $y$).
- Quadrants work **anti-clockwise.**

| | |
|---|---|
| 3 o'clock to 12 o'clock | = Quadrant 1 |
| 12 o'clock to 9 o'clock | = Quadrant 2 |
| 9 o'clock to 6 o'clock | = Quadrant 3 |
| 6 o'clock to 3 o'clock | = Quadrant 4 |

# Measures, Shape and Space

## 2D shapes

- Pentagon
  Pentagons have FIVE sides.
  Regular pentagons have FIVE EQUAL SIDES.

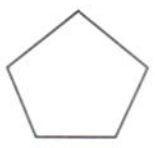

- Parallelogram
  A parallelogram is a RECTANGLE THAT HAS BEEN PUSHED OVER.
  Remember the opposite sides are the same length but parallel.

- Isosceles and scalene triangles
  An isosceles triangle has TWO EQUAL SIDES AND TWO EQUAL ANGLES.
  Picture an isosceles triangle as an arrow!

  A scalene triangle has THREE SIDES OF DIFFERENT LENGTHS and THREE ANGLES OF DIFFERENT sizes.

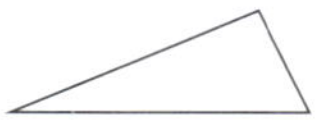

  When picturing a scalene triangle, think of SCALING A MOUNTAIN that has an easy way up or a more difficult side to climb!

## 3D shapes

- Here are some names of 3D shapes.

Cone

Cylinder

Sphere

Pyramid

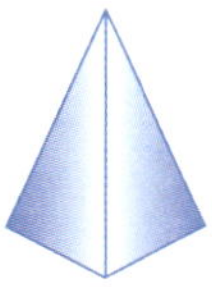

Cuboid

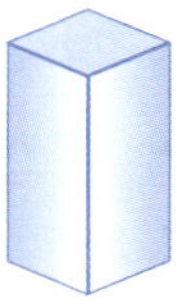

## Angles

- Acute angle = 0–89°
- Right angle = 90°
- Obtuse angle = 91–179°
- Straight line = 180°
- Reflex angle = 181–359°
- Angles around a POINT always add up to 360° (a complete turn).
- The angles of a TRIANGLE always add up to 180°.

## Symmetries

- When drawing reflections, remember to keep the correct distance from the mirror line.

## Weight and capacity

- 100 grams = 1 kilogram (100 g = 1 kg)
- 1000 kilograms = 1 ton (1000 kg = 1 ton)
- 1000 millilitres = 1 litr (1000 ml = 1 l)

## Metric and imperial conversions (approximate)

- 1 litre = 1.8 pints
- 1 kilogram = 2.2 lbs (pounds)
- 1 pound = 0.454 kg
- 1 mile = 1.6 km
- 5 miles = 8 km
- 1 foot = 30 cm
- 1 metre = 3 feet 3 inches
- 1 inch = 2.5 cm

## Estimating measures

- Milli = very small
- Centi = small
- Kilo = big

## Time

- 60 seconds = 1 minute
- 60 minutes = 1 hour
- 24 hours = 1 day
- 7 days = 1 week
- 365 days = 1 year (except a leap year which has 366 days – 2008 is a leap year)
- 52 weeks = 1 year
- 100 years = 1 century
- 1000 years = 1 millenium

## Area of a rectangle

- Area of a rectangle = length (L) × width (W)
- Area is always units squared ($cm^2$, $m^2$, $mm^2$)

# Handling Data

## Pictograms

- With pictograms PICTURE = NUMBER
  e.g.  = 20 ice creams  = 10 ice creams

## Mean, median, range, mode

- Mean = sum of all numbers divided by number of numbers
- Median = middle number in sequence (always write down in order first)
- Range = difference between highest and lowest number
- Mode = most common value

## Charts and graphs

- Be careful and accurate. Use a sharp pencil.
- Pie charts are good for percentages, fractions or decimals.

## Probability scale

- Always goes from 0 to 1 (you need fractions/decimals here).

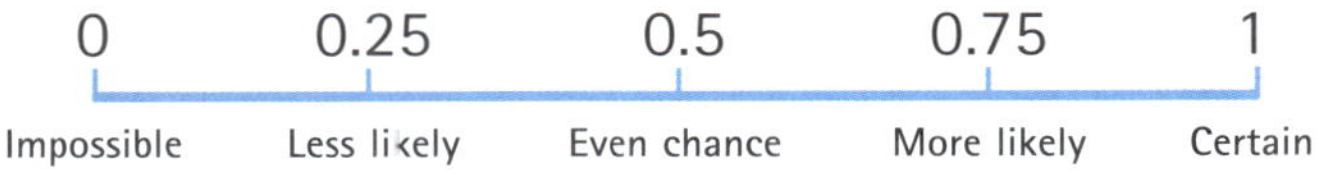

# Test techniques

## Before a test

1. When you revise, try revising a 'little and often' rather than in long sessions.
2. Learn your multiplication facts up to 10 × 10 so that you can recall them instantly. These are your tools for performing your calculations.
3. Revise with a friend. You can encourage and learn from each other.
4. Get a good night's sleep the night before.
5. Be prepared – bring your own pens and pencils and wear a watch to check the time as you go.

## During a test

1. Don't rush the first few questions. These tend to be quite straightforward, so don't make any silly mistakes.
2. As you know by now, READ THE QUESTION THEN READ IT AGAIN.
3. If you get stuck, don't linger on the same question – move on! You can come back to it later.
4. Never leave a multiple choice question. Make an educated guess if you really can't work out the answer.
5. Check to see how many marks a question is worth. Have you 'earned' those marks with your answer?
6. Check your answers. You can use the inverse method or the rounding method. Does your answer look correct?
7. Be aware of the time. After 20 minutes, check to see how far you have got.
8. Try to leave a couple of minutes at the end to read through what you have written.
9. Always show your method. You may get a mark for showing you have gone through the correct procedure even if your answer is wrong.
10. Don't leave any questions unanswered. In the two minutes you have left yourself at the end, make an educated guess at the questions you really couldn't do.

# The National Tests

## Key facts

- The Key Stage 2 National Tests (or SATs) take place in the middle of May in Year 6. You will be tested on Maths, English and Science.
- The tests take place in your school and will be marked by examiners – not your teacher!
- You will get your results in July, two months after you take the tests.
- Individual test scores are not made public but a school's combined scores are published in what are commonly known as league tables.

## The Maths National Tests

You will take three tests in Maths:

**Mental Maths Test** – This test will be played to you on a cassette. You will have to answer the questions mentally within 5, 10 or 15 seconds. This test will take about 20 minutes.

**Test A** – The non-calculator test. This test requires quick answers on a test paper. You will not be able to use a calculator but should show any working you do.

**Test B** – This test allows you to use a calculator and includes problems that will take you longer to solve.

## Don't forget!

Using and Applying Mathematics – There will be more questions testing how you use and apply your mathematical knowledge in different situations. This includes: knowing which is the important information in the questions; how to check your results; describing things mathematically using common symbols and diagrams; and explaining your reasons for conclusions that you make.

Many of the questions include elements of Using and Applying Mathematics but we have also added extra pages with specific questions designed to help you succeed in this new area of testing: pages 48 to 57.

You might be asked to explain your answers and also write possible answers. Remember, always show your method.

# Answers

**Page 8** – Decimal notation and negative numbers
1) 7 pounds and 42 pence 2) 14 pounds and 28 pence 3) 53 pounds and 71 pence
4) 109 pounds and 86 pence 5) 426 pounds and 19 pence (b) is colder

**Page 9** – Subtraction
1) 71 2) 167 3) 146 4) 138 5) 164 6) 99

**Page 10** – 2, 3, 4, 5 and 10 times table
1) 2 2) 7 3) 70 4) 9 5) 5
6) 14 7) 8 8) 80 9) 6 10) 32
11) 5 12) 5 13) 6 14) 1 15) 7

**Page 12** – Equivalent Fractions
Circled marbles $= \frac{2}{3}$ Not circled marbles $= \frac{1}{3}$

Answers will vary e.g. $\frac{2}{8} = \frac{1}{4}$ $\frac{1}{3} = \frac{2}{6}$

**Page 13** – Classifying 3D and 2D shapes

| | Cone | Cylinder | Sphere | Cuboid | Triangular-based pyramid | Triangular prism |
|---|---|---|---|---|---|---|
| Number of faces | 2 | 3 | 1 | 6 | 4 | 5 |
| Number of edges | 1 | 2 | 0 | 12 | 6 | 9 |
| Number of vertices | 1 | 0 | 0 | 8 | 4 | 6 |

**Page 14** – Tables and lists
1) Enya 2) Jessica and Enya 3) Jessica and Thomas

**Page 15** – Bar charts and pictograms
1) tuna mayonnaise 2) 7 3) 18

**Page 16** – Short addition
1) 8493 2) 899 3) 2080 4) 11 979

**Page 17** – Short subtraction
1) 7951 2) 6188 3) 7960 4) 2525

**Page 18** – Decimals
1) 15.11 2) 123.3 km 3) £15.92 4) 8.56 5) 1.28 6) 38.84 km

**Page 19** – Decimals
1) 1.77, 7.87, 8.7, 8.87, 18.28 2) 2.55 km, 5.22 km, 25.52 km, 55.2 km
3) 9.224, 9.242, 9.424, 9.442, 9.99 4) 0.077, 0.73, 0.734, 0.773

**Page 21** – Multiplying and dividing by 10 and 100
1) 650 2) 10 3) 100 4) 42 200
5) 17 6) 10 7) 10 8) 70

**Page 22** – Short multiplication
1) 2550 2) 2852 3) 1995 4) 2534 5) 6957 6) 5112

**Page 23** – Short division
1) 48 2) 78 r1 3) 297 4) 91 r 6

**Page 24** – Number patterns
1) 0 and 10. Rule is 'add 5'. 2) 34 and 85. Rule is 'add 17' 3) 141, 72 and 49. Rule is 'subtract 23'.

**Page 25** – Number patterns
1) 32: 1, 2, 4, 8, 16, 32
2) 60: 1, 2, 3, 4, 5, 6, 10, 12, 15, 20, 30, 60
3) 42: 1, 2, 3, 6, 7, 14, 21, 42
4) 80: 1, 2, 4, 5, 8, 10, 16, 20, 40, 80

Prime numbers 2, 3, 5, 7, 11, 13, 17, 19, 23, 29, 31, 37, 41, 43, 47, 53, 59, 61, 67, 71, 73, 79, 83, 89, 91, 97

**Page 26** – Checking your answers
1) 457 check 457 + 67 = 524
2) 40 check 40 × 4 = 160
3) 6987 check 6987 + 897 = 7884
4) 45 check 45 × 50 = 2250

1) 7557 Rough answer = 700 × 10 = 7000
2) 283 Rough answer 400 – 100 = 300
3) 26 Rough answer 460 ÷ 20 = 23

**Page 27** – Checking your answers
1011 / In his first calculation, Billy put 112 instead of 12 into his calculator. 435 × 112 = 48,720

**Page 28** – Recognising proportions of a whole
1) dog
2) 30

**Page 29** – Recognising proportions of a whole

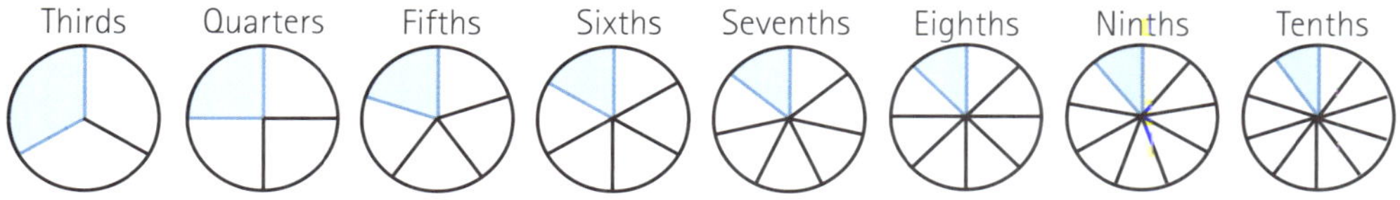


**Page 30** – Using coordinates
1) (4, 1); (2, 5) and (6, 5)
2) (a) Phantom Hill (b) Carnage Cliff (c) Pirate Point

**Page 31** – Using coordinates
Answers will vary

**Page 32** – 3D shapes – making models

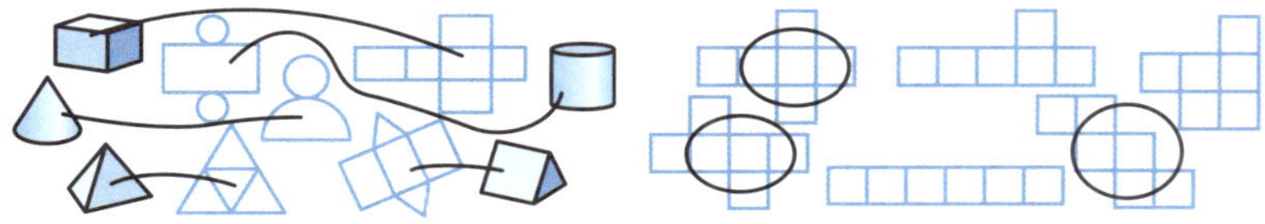

**Page 33** – 3D shapes – making models
First example needs 8 blocks to complete the cuboid
Second example needs 8 blocks to complete the cuboid

**Page 34** – 2D shapes
Answers will vary

**Page 35** – 2D shapes

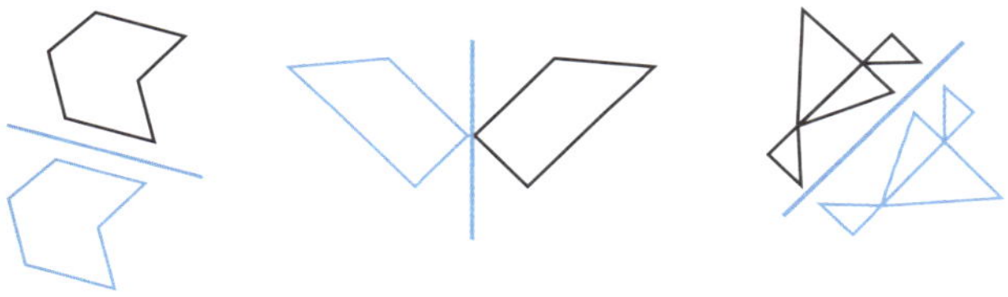

**Page 38** – Measures
1) Your foot, DVD case
2) Glass of milk, can of cola
3) Scales
4) Ruler
5) Answers will vary. Use chart to check answers.

**Page 40** – Grouping data
1) 2
2) 6
3) 6 – 10
4) 12
5) No they didn't

**Page 42** – Line graphs
1) June, 8500 surfboards were sold.
2) February and March
3) July and August
4) June, July and August
5) Could be bought as Christmas presents.

**Page 43** – Line graphs
1) 5 2) August and September 3) 3 places

**Page 44** – Finding the range
19 341 books

**Page 45** – Finding the mode
Mode = 2

**Page 47** – Using simple formulae
1) £9 2) 5 3) £4
A = (J × 9) + 3

**Page 51** – Solving number problems
1) The candles were £18
2) The fondue set was £25
3) Baz and Gaz shortchange ' Eadcase by 10p so 'Eadcase 'Arry will do one of two things, depending on his mood:
(a) Let Baz and Gaz be the first to 'try-out' the new butchers' block and fondue set.
(b) Make them put all the flat-pack furniture together and redecorate the hideout in a nice shade of peach.

**Page 53** – Solving measures problems

1) 1600 cups of punch 2) 1968 m or 1.968 km 3) Billy Biceps lifts 201.5 kg 4) 8072 litres
5) 24 revolutions per ride 6) 4.95 kg or 4950 grams of food

**Page 55** – Solving shape and space problems

1) 27 2) 22 3) 24 ways

**Page 56** – Solving data handling problems
Venn Diagram – flow chart

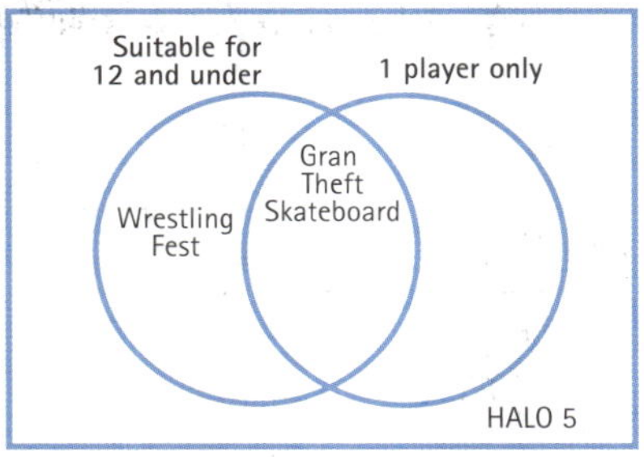


**Page 57** – Solving data handling problems
1) Multiples of 7 = 7, 14, 21
Even numbers = 2, 4, 6, 8, 10, 12, 14, 16, 18, 20, 22, 24
The answer is 14

2) Square numbers = 16, 25, 36, 49
Two-digit numbers = 12, 15, 18, 21, 24, 27, 30, 33, 36, 39, 42, 45, 48
The answer is 36

3) A/B/C/D/E/F/A or the reverse of this are the only two solutions.

4) 10 handshakes

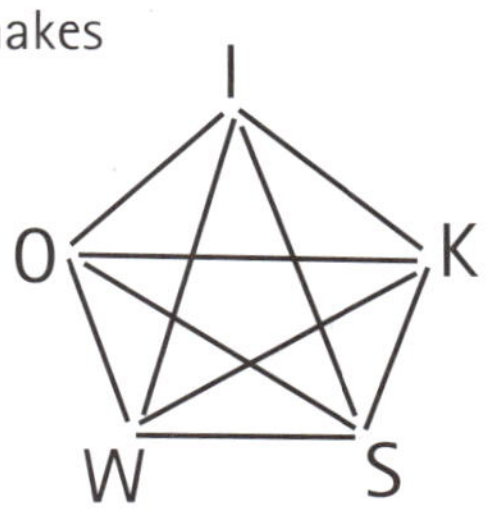